Getting Your Slice

of the

Pie

A DEFINITIVE SOURCE FOR PROSPERING IN PIZZA

Tracy Powell

Empowered Innovations
Jeffersonville, Indiana

Getting Your Slice of the Pie
A Definitive Source for Prospering in Pizza
By Tracy Powell

Published by:

Empowered Innovations

2405 Kingsfield St.
Jeffersonville, IN 47130-9575 U.S.A.
getmyslice@pizzaprosperity.com
www.pizzaprosperity.com

Publisher's Cataloging-in-Publication Data

Powell, Tracy
    Getting your slice of the pie: a definitive source for prospering in pizza / Tracy Powell
        p. cm.
    Includes index.
    ISBN: 0-9709195-0-6
    LCCN: 2001012345
        1. Business—United States—Reference—Directories.
        2. Market analysis—United States—International.   I. Title.

Cover design by Empowered Innovations

Printed in the United States of America

10 9 8 7 6 5 4 3 2

Word Has It ...

"This book is a necessary tool for understanding your pizza business. Avoid thinking that just beause you've been around for 25 years that you won't relate to this. Whether you're a startup, or next generation, or eyeing chain expansion, there is something in this book that you will need to know."
    Vince Cianfichi, owner of Vince the Pizza Prince, Scranton, PA

"For a change, this book is not about pizza recipes; it is about the recipe of success in managing your pizza business, for both independent and chain operators."
    Antoine Bakhache, CEO and co-founder of Pizza Corner, India

"As a pizza operator for roughly 30 years, and my father's 40 years at the business, we find that Mr. Powell has done a real good job of presenting what the world of pizza has and will evolve to."
    Rocky Rice, co-owner of Swing-In Pizza, Bloomington, IN

"The prayers of want-to-be pizza entrepreneurs have been answered. Finally a conscise and easy-to-read collection of information and introduction to the pizza industry. Written in a fresh and lively format, entrepreneurs considering the rewards and opportunities in the world of pizza will appreciate having such a complete resource available to them.
    "For about the cost of a couple of large pizzas, you can learn more about the pizza industry than you could learn in a week of phone calls and lunches. A very welcome and authoritative volume written by someone who truly has their finger on the pulse of the industry."
    Robin Weinrich, Sirius Technologies

"This book is most certainly written by a person who's been right down there in the trenches. It provides a very readable overview of the nitty gritty of the pizza business. Filled with instructive anecdotes that any insider would recognize, it also informs newcomers about what they'll need to consider, should they join the industry."
    Drew McCarthy, Editor, Canadian Pizza Magazine

This book is dedicated to those pizza professionals who have given jobs to most of us reading this book. Without their innovations and boundless determination, pizza would not be the dynamic industry as we know it. My hats off to you all, and to all those who follow in their footsteps.

Acknowledgments

Clearly without the support of my wife, Cristine, this book wouldn't have stood a chance of being produced. Time is the most precious commodity we possess, and she sacrificed plenty of it to allow this dream to become reality.

Disclaimer

There's quite a bit of information packed into these pages, some of which contains advice, tips and observations. This book is designed to provide information on pizza restaurant operations and pizza industry analysis. It's sold with the understanding that the publisher and author are not engaged in rendering legal, accounting or other professional services.

This book's purpose isn't to reprint all the information that's otherwise available, but instead to complement, amplify and supplement other texts. You're encouraged to read all the available material, learn as much as possible about pizzeria operations, and tailor the information to your individual needs.

Opening and operating a pizza restaurant is not a get-rich-quick scheme. Anyone who decides to run an operation must expect to invest a lot of time and effort into it.

Every effort has been made to make this book as complete and as accurate as possible. However, there may be mistakes, both typographical and in content; therefore, this text should be used only as a general guide and not as the ultimate source of pizzeria operations and industry analysis. Also, this book contains information that is current only up to the printing date.

The purpose of this book is to enlighten, educate and entertain. The author and Empowered Innovations will have neither liability nor responsibility to any person or entity with respect to any loss or damage caused, or alleged to have been caused, directly or indirectly, by the information contained in this book.

Contents

Introduction

This Book's Birthing Pains (But It's So Cute!)

The purpose for writing this book is the same purpose pizza plays in today's food service marketplace: pizza came to be because there was a gaping need. The only difference is that pizza fills gaping mouths, whereas this book fills gaping minds in search of inside information within the oft-elusive pizza industry.

I've attempted to answer many of the questions I hear time and again as an editorial staffer with Pizza Today, the industry's premier trade magazine, a common one resembling "I want to open a pizza restaurant ... where do I begin?" Obviously, every person asking a question along this vein is at a different point in his or her quest to pizza stardom, a different stage in professional or entrepreneurial pursuit.

So the usual answer I offer is to educate oneself. But aside from suggesting they read a couple of back issues of our magazine, attend a trade show or two (we also coordinate and host the world's largest pizza events, Pizza Expo‰) and study some statistics I've compiled, these eager people remain uninformed of what it takes to run a pizzeria. Thus the reason behind "Getting Your Slice of the Pie": to educate, enlighten and encourage those who have considered opening a pizzeria of their own.

Educating entrepreneurial minds in any new venture in the industry in which they're setting their sights is one of the basic tenets of any reputable business school. Going into a new business blind is like walking the plank, only you don't know what's awaiting you below. So the need I'm addressing isn't anything new, but it is unique—no other mass market book has been made available with such insight. After reading this book, you will be equipped with a working knowledge of pizza operations, particularly in what you will need to purchase before and during your pizzeria's life, what food ingredients and styles will make your shop tick, and what special needs are associated with an establishment primarily selling pizza.

Enlightenment comes in discovering some shop secrets. For an industry filled with such open-minded, creative and personal souls, there's a lot of secrecy surrounding what makes one player better than another. In these pages you're going to find out, not only what you can do operationally to virtually guarantee the public's love affair with your pizza, but what the trends are.

It is my hope that you will be encouraged, too. Opening a restaurant can seem to be quite a daunting task—and it is, to be sure! But the rewards are incredible, if you take care to succeed. After reading "Getting Your Slice of the Pie" it is my sincere wish that I have planted some seeds of success in your heart and mind, and that you'll rise to the top of the industry, as others have. Yes, they've made plenty of money, many of them now millionaires. Remember that you are no different than any of the wildly successful and profitable pizziaolos that have ever come along. When you read about some of the top pizza people that have shaped the industry, picture yourself in their shoes (and aprons), because there's nothing stopping you from achieving the same—if not much better—results.

I must admit that, before you plunge into the material, my good tidings have another side. Many have come and gone in the pizza industry, sold on making a quick buck, and have left behind an empty shell of a building and a bad taste in their neighborhood's minds and mouths. They are the ones that bought cheap and sold cheap, without much concern of quality and service. I truly believe that the day has come when pizza is on the verge of being bumped to the next level, and it might as well be bumped up by you. With an eye on superior quality product and top-notch customer service, it is also my intent to usher in a new era of pizza stars. How hundreds, possibly thousands, of earnest entrepreneurs with the correct tools and intentions will improve on an already outstanding industry I don't know.

But I do know I'm excited to be a part of it!

What this book is not about

If you're looking for a book on pizza recipes, you won't find them here. That is, except in the resource section near the end, where I point you in the direction of other authors. Pizza cookbooks and recipes are plentiful, and while informative, I've chosen to dwell on other aspects of the restaurant.

This is also not a write-up on some of the more intricate aspects on starting your own business. Again, wonderful references are listed in the resource section. The modus operandi of start-ups can be accessed in a variety of other publications, and I suggest you cover this topic in depth if this is your first business venture.

"Getting Your Slice of the Pie" deals exclusively with what it takes to dive into the pizza business, with topics given considerable space that I feel will best benefit you, the potential pizza potentate. There are many other aspects to consider, as with any other business, once up and running (thus the reason for Pizza Today's popularity). And maybe, if I start receiving enough inquiries (or hate mail), there will be another book.

My right to write

Beginning this book grew out of, as stated before, the basic economic principle of meeting a need. Am I the final authority on everything pizza? Certainly not—in fact, I've listed a group of my close associates deep in the industry, and with many more years on me, in the resource section. These folks are adept consultants who have helped many around the world become the industry's success stories. No, I just happen to be a lover of pizza, a lover of people, and a lover of words, put in a position of autonomy where most haven't found themselves.

Over 10 years I managed multiple Pizza Huts for two franchises and corporate, working my way up from a cook position, with numerous contacts with independent operators along the way. Now, as associate editor for Pizza Today since 1999, I find myself in an ideal situation to bring fresh and unbiased insight into the world of pizza. Unbiased is the key word, as the industry is fraught with hard-line competition among equipment manufacturers, differing operational concepts and styles, and, of course, the pizza itself.

Taking a cue from my position, then, I offer you an opportunity to learn what the pros know. That is, what commercial pizza is all about. I hope you take this information and use it as a springboard to make your next million dollars.

Why This Book Is Necessary For Your Success

There are currently 23 million small business owners in the United States. Chances are, because your reading this book, you are either one of these 23 million, or you soon will be.

The optimism of the American entrepreneur is not without foundation. In a recent Gallup study commissioned by the National Federation of Independent Businesses (NFIB) there were about 3.5 million new business startups in 1995.

And though statistics can be used to prove anything, even the most conservative figures put new business starts at over 700,000 per year for the past three years. Bill Gardner, economist with University of Southern California Entrepreneurship Program, says that this level of startups has not been seen in over 100 years. The downside is that as many as 50 percent of these businesses will not make it past their first year.

In fact, in 1999, 528,000 small businesses were shuttered. Over 4,000 of them were pizzerias.

Such enlightening numbers to throw your way in the outset of this book! Sort of like reading morbid news headlines before your first cup of coffee. Actually, I'm setting up a contrast—a challenge, really, as most people in pizza seem to shine in the face of adversity.

The singular purpose for "Getting Your Slice of the Pie" is to help people be successful. I want everyone who works hard to succeed. I want to give people new ideas and models based on the successes of people just like them. I want to lift them up and give them inspiration when they feel like quitting. I want to give them hope and strength. "Getting Your Slice of the Pie" is the only how-to book focusing on the fundamentals of the industry, to be used when starting and growing a pizza business. Although there are resources out there for the present pizza pro, there are none for the beginner *and* the pizza pro. Even the few volumes written with the pizza professional in mind have become antiquated, without solutions to today's unique business challenges.

The special facet of this book is that it's written for you. Too much of the day is often spent squelching fires and handling the stressful aspects of the business, from personnel issues to customer complaints to vendor relations. While this is part and parcel to holding the position of a business leader, a light approach to these issues, one that's unbiased yet with an inside edge, is a cool raindrop on a hot summer day. It's good for the soul. You deserve it.

And that's my desire for your use of "Getting Your Slice of the Pie", among other things. Pizza is fun food; it's also fun business. Don't be one of the stats and allow your business to fail, whether a slow death or a quick tragedy. Dive into the following pages with a never-say-never attitude, an empowered belief that you're in to succeed, not fail; to win, not lose.

With such positive thoughts, this book will play a vital role in your current and future prosperity in the pizza industry, no matter at what level you find yourself.

Share this book with your associates, your managers, your employees, and you'll see other questions answered which you hadn't entertained. There are usually some basic questions lingering in the back of employees' and supervisors' minds that never surface, whether due to fear of embarrassment or the inability to put them into words.

This volume covers a broad range of issues, and should answer most of them. The bonus is: no one risks feeling stupid by asking! (I can see someone now, hiding in the back corner by the flour rack, peeking through the pages.)

The People Proponent to Pizza Prosperity

As completion of "Getting Your Slice of the Pie" quickly neared, I asked for input from various operators and chain execs. Much to my chagrin, I was shown the area of most importance, an area that permeates every level of pizza production and operations—the people. People are such an integral part of our highly successful industry that I overlooked the obvious!

But the more I contemplated where to include extrapolating on how critical the "people factor" is in the pizza industry, the clearer I saw that you can't put it in a box, or a chapter. This subject is a book in and of itself! Instead, as most business leaders know—even if not in so many words, the People Proponent is a broad-based, living organism that exists in every facet of operations.

The People Proponent is behind every section of this book, and every one that I don't touch on. Even now, as I write this outside of the four walls of a store, this proponent of success spurs me on in order to help people.

People fuel the engine that powers the various dynamics that drives our industry. People we call customers pay our salaries; people we call employees cook and serve our product; people we call supervisors lead the employees to achieve success at unit and market levels; people we call peers relate to our frustrations and offer support. Not focusing on the critical area of understanding and properly treating people on all these levels leads only to a dead-end, and you're sure to fail.

But, you say, isn't this true in any service-oriented

industry? Yes and no. Yes, due to obvious reasons: people serve people, and it takes people to pay for services rendered or product sold—the majestic current called capitalism at its most basic working definition.

In the same breath I'll tell you that the pizza industry is unique, that the people proponent is even more prevalent, even compared to other foodservice concepts. At its very nature, there exists the people factor. Think back to what pizza means to you, even before you were out of grade school. It was fun, it was exciting, there was usually activity surrounding it. Don't blink here—you might miss this: pizza is people-oriented, and it's ingrained in your internal wiring. And that's not true just for you—it's true for your vendors, it's true for your customers, your employees. Everybody relates pizza—not just the food, but the experience—with other people.

Therefore, the most important ingredient for success in the pizza industry is healthy dose of people skills. And it must either be hammered into you (and those working with and around you), or you're blessed and have been born with it. Understand people, and how to fulfill needs, and you're on your way to prospering in pizza.

1

Are You Primed For Pizza?

Before there was Pizza Hut, the world's largest pizza chain, there were two brothers, the Carneys, with no food background and no money of their own. Before there was Dominos Pizza, the second largest chain, there was Tom Monaghan, a young, shy small-town guy with big dreams. Before there was Papa John's, now the third biggest, there was a kid making pizza in the broom closet of his dad's bar.

What do these guys have in common with you? You share a desire to make and serve pizza out of your own restaurant, to call yourself the proprietor of your own pizza shop, the creator of your own menu, and the leader of people. Other things are common as well, in varying degrees: a deep-down desire to please others, to see a smile when they eat one of your pizzas; an innate need to interact with the public; the love of creating signature dishes and unique products; and, like most successful entrepreneurs, a vision.

There are stories like that of Buddy LaRosa. He started out in 1954 with $300, renting a storefront in Cincinnati for $125 a month, and putting a down payment on an oven. Unable to afford a mixer in those early years, LaRosa was forced to go to a nearby bakery every night to make 30 pounds of dough for the next day. Today, some 40 years later, his vision is a living one—he's got the Cincinnati market by the tail, with 53 LaRosa's stores in that area.

I visited the original store once and was blown away. Walking through the dining room was one thing—signed photos of local legend Pete Rose, diplomats and celebrities lined the walls, an integrated deli and grocery store under the same roof—but checking out the back of the house was another. The size of the kitchen was like that of a commercial bakery, loaded with sets of ovens and make stations. There's no question LaRosa is a pizza success story, one that's bound to be his legacy.

Then there's the next generation of pizza leaders; one example is seen in the founders of East of Chicago Pizza. Six guys fresh out of college (four of them fraternity brothers) delved into pizza in 1990 and haven't looked back since. At mid-year 2000, their company ran or had franchised 122 units. In 1999, their company had sales exceeding $54 million.

Even Generation Y is getting a piece of the action. There was a report of a 16-year-old in Hartford, Kentucky who bought an existing pizzeria with the backing of his father. He had begun the restaurant life bussing tables when he was 9, and liked the business so much he wanted in for life.

I'm convinced that out there somewhere is the next LaRosa, the next Frank Carney, the next Tom Monaghan, the next John Schnatter—I could list about 5,000 other success stories of fabulously inventive and equally successful one-and-two-shop operators, rich in their own right. The next success story may be a person working in a pizzeria right now. It may be a restaurant manager in the burger industry, wanting to switch to a faster-growing segment. It may be a person with an entrepreneural spirit that simply loves to eat pizza. It may be you.

But jumping in, adrenaline pumping, with eyes glazed over will either bring certain failure or a slow, painful death to your startup and your dreams. Knowing pizza is essential to long-term success, and that begins with a book like this—a manual, if you will, shedding some light on what awaits you so you'll know what to be prepared for. If you're not convinced that basic pizza information is this valuable, consider the foodservice smarts of Max & Erma's and McDonald's.

Max & Erma's is a family-style restaurant that had 1999 revenues of $108.6 million—certainly no small timer in the world of food. In '98 they began a concept called Ironwood Cafe that featured hardwood-fired pizza ovens. Little over a year later they closed the three they'd opened at a loss of $2 million. An analyst for Hilliard Lyons told the press that the concept was good on paper, but the execution was poor. In other words, they didn't know pizza as a whole package—preparation, baking, presentation, branding, marketing ... the list goes on.

McDonald's saw its pizza venture, the McPizza, flop in the mid-1980s, due to, again, poor execution. Recently, the fast food giant is back in the game thanks to its strategic acquisition of a regional Columbus, Ohio-based chain, Donatos. Since then a Happy Meal has seen a personal cheese pizza in the bag. The expertise of one of the country's best-quality pizza players, found in Donatos, was certainly worth quite a bit of money and interest on the part of the burger segment. It's still too early to tell how successful the pizza sales are in today's McD's.

For these two companies, failure with one idea or another is simply written off—they take a small (to them) hit, and move on. The company as a whole survives. You, on the other hand, probably don't have the financial backing for such mistakes. Thus the importance of knowing pizza inside and out, and one of the driving reasons behind this book.

Reasons Behind the Popularity of Pizza

So what makes pizza so popular? Is it price point? Is it because it's so easily delivered, one of the only foods that "hold up" well during transport in a cardboard box? Yes to all the above, and then a few other reasons. In fact, learning what's behind the mass public's love for pizza is a key to understanding how to make, market and present your end product.

First off, pizza is a communal food. The entire restaurant industry has shifted back toward this valuable concept, after gearing more toward fast food and quick service in the past decade or so. You're seeing more and more restaurants offering "family meals", even going so far in some American-style full-service concerns as selling serving bowls of items like mashed potatoes and corn. Even carryout is becoming more family-oriented—Taco Bell offers family packs, KFC (like many chicken chains) for a long time has offered family portions, including buckets of chicken.

It's interesting to see the public's interest in a desire to return to "how things used to be" to recapture a sense of family values, while at the same time becoming more time-strapped and inclined to instant gratification. Enter pizza, the perfect food for the times.

By its very nature, pizza is eaten slice by slice from one pan or from one box. Even if you're throwing a party, everyone gathers at one spot—where the pizzas are—to get his or her portion. This makes pizza a fun food, while also fulfilling a deep desire for community, whether with family or friends.

Versatility is another icon of convenience. Pepperoni pizza, or one with extra cheese, is an old friend—simple and cheaper than other pies on the menu, you ordered it when you were a kid, and you continue to order it late at night when you're in socks and sweats. Yet you can dress pizza up if you're throwing a party, ordering one or each type to be sure to please everybody. You're even able to order "half and half" for discriminating tastes—just cheese on one half, loaded on the other.

May I suggest allowing customers the option of "special ordering"? By special ordering, I mean the half-and-half orders, the orders that replace one topping for another with a pie that has certain ingredients (i.e., a meat pie that's topped with pepperoni, ham, sausage and beef)—anything that's requested which changes the normal production specs on a pizza. Avoid charging extra for such requests, or making it difficult for the customer; avoid it like the plague. Versatility is akin to convenience in the pizza consumer's mind, and complicating this given may mean losing the person's business. Happily honoring these requests will only cost you pennies in the short term, and earn loyalty long term.

There are also variations in crust. Various crusts are

more popular than others in each region of the country. Chicago natives love deep dish and stuffed pizza. New Yorkers can't live without their thin crust. But with a shrinking national and worldwide community, more crusts have been introduced to the four corners of the globe, and it's safe to say that some New Yorkers secretly like a thicker, chewy crust (although you'd be hard-pressed to hear one admit it). It may prove profitable to provide more than one type of crust, depending on what demand there is in your area.

Portability also accounts for pizza's popularity—look no further than the statistics on carryout and delivery in The Status of the Industry Report, in the back section of this book. Pizza is a fairly durable product (if prepared and cooked correctly) and withstands the rigors of delivery (again, if done correctly). Much effort has gone into the science behind keeping a pizza hot while in the box and while in the delivery pouch. Due diligence in seeking out the latest technologies and understanding issues of transporting pizza from the shop to the home will pay off.

Then there's the fat factor, which sings to the world's palate. Indulgence food, like chocolate, ice cream and potato chips—and pizza—is so appetizing because, quite simply, it tastes good. Our mouths water like Pavlov's dog's when we think about our favorite indulgence. The reason is that fat blends flavors and times the release of flavor compounds naturally present in food. Without the presence of fat, the flavor explosion our taste buds crave isn't there. The taste of most low-fat or no-fat products is either dull, or you can taste individual ingredients—the salt, the pepper, for instance.

This isn't to say low-fat pizzas are out of the question for your menu, or that they're vastly unpopular. In fact, with the consistent rise of health consciousness, it's wise to put a few healthful items on your menu. But be aware that, as far as the pizza lover's palate is concerned, fat is where it's at!

There's even a breakdown on what people are more inclined to crave in terms of fat and taste. Studies have shown that men 40 and older love fat-salt mixtures like nachos, hamburgers, hot dogs and pizza. Women 40 and older usually crave fat-sugar mixtures like cakes, donuts, pies or chocolate.

Teens and kids crave anything tasty, which is good for the pizza industry, since many times they're the ones clamoring for pizza for dinner and parents go along.

Today's Market Growth, Tomorrow's Market Growth

For a better understanding of the pizza industry as a whole, realize that pizza is in its adolescence, at least in America.

In its infancy, the origins of ancient pizza can be traced back to about 1000 B.C., when the Etruscans arrived in northern and central parts of Italy from Asia Minor. These early pizza lovers made pizza (minus any tomatoes) with a focaccia crust. Another form, probably the world's first thin crust pie, was made by the Egyptians around the same time. It was baked on heated stones.

A bit more recently, the first known pizzeria, Port Alba in Naples, opened in 1830 and is still open today. In those days, pizza was the grub of the poorer Neoapolitans, putting whatever they could find on a crust for breakfast, lunch and dinner.

The first pizza delivery was made in 1889 by Don Raffaele Esposito, owner of the Pietro il Pizzalolo in Naples. By then, pizza had gained in popularity in the area, and the first delivery was ordered by visiting Queen Margherita Teresa Giovanni, the consort of King Umberto I (the king of Italy). Refusing to go to a low-class pizza shop, yet excited to try what everyone was talking about, the queen ordered in. (The pizza featured tomatoes, mozzarella cheese—a cheese never before used til then—and basil, ingredients bearing the colors red, white and green for the Italian flag. This is the birth of the modern-day tomato-and-cheese pizza. You'll still find Margherita pizzas on menus around the world with these same ingredients.)

The first American pizzeria opened in New York on 53 $^{1/2}$ Spring St. in 1905. During World War II, U.S. servicemen experienced pizza while stationed in Europe, and brought their new cravings back home. One indicator of the mass acceptance of this new food in the states is seen in oregano sales during this period: sales increased 5,200 percent between 1948 and 1956.

One of these servicemen was a man named John Bender, whom I had the privilege of working for during my days at Indiana University. Ever wonder how the Carney brothers learned to make pizza? In brief, the story goes: Frank and Dan Carney was approached by a family friend with the idea of opening a pizza parlor, and, after borrowing $600 from their mother, they opened the first Pizza Hut in 1958. The family friend was John Bender. He brought his passion for pizza back from the war zone, making pies for neighbors every week out of his home. In fact, looking at an old, small building on a street corner in Wichita, Kansas, which had a hanging sign too small for much verbiage, it was John's wife who said, in so many words: "The building looks like a hut, and there's not much room on the sign for much else—let's just call it Pizza Hut."

Shortly afterward, Domino's began its delivery legacy in 1960, and pizza swept the country, a region at a time. And today, commercial pizza is in every developed country (Pizza Hut, the leader in international expansion, is in 87 countries).

And it's actually on the international front that companies both great and small are seeing awesome opportunities and lands of plenty. South American countries, once thought too poor to support a pizza enterprise, are now welcoming the likes of Pizza Hut and Domino's. (One hot market is Brazil, where 80-unit Mr. Pizza is bracing for American chain expansion and some new competition.) Latin America has been the target for Papa John's for a few years now, and the Middle East is beginning to be sprinkled with chain players.

Twenty-three-unit Pizza Corner has had the handle on India for a few years now, and is now going head to head with Domino's there as the native Indian chain plans to open 100 more units over the next four years. Little Caesars inked a deal recently to open 300 stores in Mexico. China is a market that's being explored lately, and with great success. Louisville, Kentucky-based Bearno's, a 23-unit chain, recently signed a franchise deal to open 40 stores within the confines of the Great Wall. Pizza Inn's open in Iceland and has 20 locations in The United Arab Emirates. There seems to be more and more borders being opened—the opportunity is profitable enough for Domino's to focus its expansion plans this year overseas, not in the states.

One interesting story is that of Mad Maddy's Italian Kitchens, a gourmet-style pizza group found only in the Boston and Los Angeles areas. Beginning this year, and continuing through 2006, the company's looking to open five units in Honolulu, 11 units in China, 18 in Japan, three in Vietnam, eight in Taiwan, five in Indonesia, four in Hong Kong, 16 in Korea, four in Malaysia, four in Thailand, and three in Singapore. Such targeted expansion plans are ones to watch and possibly follow, especially considering that Mad Maddy's has been relative homebodies for the last 30 years. Something must have incited the company to sell pies on foreign soil, and it's my guess it's the same as everyone else's—sales.

So let me do my part and pass along some information on one part of the world many other American pizzaiolos are flocking to: Europe. Space not permitting, I'll only divulge information on a few of the key countries to give you a taste of what's on the other side of the Big Pond.

First know that the latest trend in dining out in Europe is the fast casual concept, combining speed and productivity with new culinary products. Think along the lines of Fazoli's, or California Pizza Kitchen's CPK ASAP (the scaled-down express-style CPK). Let's take the French market as one example. France's pizza segment's sales growth has been 9% over the last couple of years, and was led by Pizza Pai with an 18.6% sales growth to 65.1 million euros in 1999. Pizza Hut had 132 units in France with 122.1 million euros in sales, and Pizza del Arte has 69 outlets with 61.7 million in sales.

Ireland is pretty saturated with pubs and steakhouses, but seems to like pizza, too. There's just not a lot of players to offer it—a market that may be ripe, taken also that the country has the youngest population in Europe. The top dogs in Ireland are: Supermac's (a concept that sells burgers, chicken and pizza) with 43 stores; Four Star Pizza with 20 units; Pizza Hut with 12; Apache Pizza, 9; Domino's, 5. Some analysts speculate that there are few chain pizza stores because the Republic of Ireland is a smaller country with a tendency to support independent outlets.

In the United Kingdom, Pizza Express holds an approximate 24% market share with over 220 stores, clearly the leader. It's also an aggressive franchisor outside of the British isles; franchisees that are abroad include those in Egypt, Russia, Poland, Pakistan and Turkey. The main competition includes Caffe Uno, Est Est Est, Ask, Tortellini and Pizza Piazza. In the U.K., fast-food outlets account for a greater proportion of sales than anywhere else in Europe.

Spain is the home stomping grounds of TelePizza, the dominant delivery chain in the country. TelePizza owns or franchises more than 760 units, and has a presence in seven other countries as well. The company's known for their fleet of 15,000 mopeds, used to deliver pies in the tight streets in European cities.

Some interesting things to note about European countries:

♦   Meals remain the central focus of the day for residents of France, Spain and Belgium. Full-service eateries remain in demand, while fast-food is largely out. Carryout is a fairly recent phenomenon in France.

♦   Spain and Italy have strong cafe and carryout sectors—Italy with the highest proportion of carryout per inhabitant. But the love for the independent operator is a strong root in the society, and few chains have dared planting stakes there.

   ◆   The European market share is divvied up primarily among the following countries: (in number of outlets) U.K. 19%; Italy 19%; Germany 18%; Spain 18%; France 16%; Belgium 4%; Netherlands 4%; Republic of Ireland 2%.

Also, if you're seriously considering the international idea, you'll want to know how difficult it is to find workers. Here's the latest unemployment rates:

Japan	3.7%
Norway	4.1%
Netherlands	5.1%
Austria	4.4%
New Zealand	6.7%
Portugal	6.2%
Australia	8.2%
U.K.	7.3%
Denmark	5.8%
Ireland	9.5%
Canada	8.9%
Sweden	5.8%
Germany	9.1%
Belgium	9.5%
France	11.8%
Italy	12.1%
Finland	12.8%
Greece	9.9%
Spain	20.1%

Source: FoodService Europe

Compare these to the current U.S. rate of 4.5%.

Going down under for pizza is nothing new—pizza is the only segment nearing saturation in the Australian market. The restaurant scene is vibrant in Australia, and has been for some time now. Pizza Hut leads the charge with 400 units, Pizza Haven (an Aussie concept) has 220, Domino's has 140, and Eagle Boys Pizza (also Aussie) also has 140.

Closer to home, Canada is becoming a burgeoning land of pizza. Pizza Hut is currently muscling in with its might, the largest Canadian-born chain being Toronto-based Pizza Pizza with 320 units and $70 million in 2000 sales.

Where Do You Fit In?

That's the real question. But it's not a question with negative connotations. Yes, there are companies that have the lion's share of the pizza-consuming market. Currently, the Big Four (Pizza Hut, Dominos, Little Caesar's and Papa John's) command 47% of the U.S. pizza market in terms of sales, but take heart—there's good news for the person wanting to purchase a franchise with a leader and the one wishing to run his own shop. Consider this: a Leading Edge report estimated that chain sales would increase from $15.8 billion in '98 to $18.4 billion in 2003, and independents sales would see a jump from $8.9 billion to $10.4 billion.

Those who prophesy that the pizza market is becoming saturated are short-sighted (see the 'U.S. Market Saturation Report in the back of the book). If young John Schnatter had believed the skeptics 16 years ago, he would have either not began Papa John's, or at least been content with one or two stores. Sixteen years ago, Pizza Hut had a much larger market share.

So the answer to the question is: you'll fit in where you want to fit in, granted you make the right moves at the outset, and execute properly once you're there. Pizza has become so widely popular that, if you provide exceptional service and quality, consistent product, you're going to succeed. There are even some hot markets that, given you're on the right street, increase your chances:

10 Best Large Metro Areas to Start a Business
1.   Phoenix, Arizona
2.   Salt Lake City-Provo, Utah
3.   Atlanta, Georgia
4.   Raleigh-Durham, North Carolina
5.   Indianapolis, Indiana
6.   Dallas-Fort Worth, Texas
7.   Charlotte, North Carolina
8.   Memphis, Tennessee
9.   Washington, D.C.
10.   Orlando, Florida

10 Best Small Metro Areas to Start a Business
1.   Las Vegas, Nevada
2.   Fargo-Moorehead, North Dakota
3.   Sioux Falls, South Dakota
4.   Reno, Nevada
5.   Austin, Texas
6.   Charleston, South Carolina
7.   Wilmington-Jacksonville, North Carolina
8.   Montgomery, Alabama
9.   Columbia, South Carolina
10.   Baton Rouge, Louisiana

*Source: *Inc.* magazine's rankings based on the 2000 edition of Entrepreneurial Hot Spots: The Best Places in America to Start and

Grow a Company, produced by economic-research firm Cognetics, Inc. Those areas above that ranked on this list had a large number of significant business start-ups and the local economy was able to support the growth of a most of them.

Other regions not listed above, ones to keep an eye on, are the areas that grew by leaps and bounds this past decade. Keep in mind that the population of the entire country grew at a 13.2% rate over the same period of time.

❀   Naples, Florida: 65.3% population growth from 1990-2000

❀   Yuma, Arizona: 49.7% growth

❀   McAllen-Edinburg-Mission, Texas: 48.5%

❀   Fayetteville-Springdale-Rogers, Arkansas: 47.5%

❀   Boise City, Idaho: 46.1%

❀   Laredo, Texas: 44.9%

❀   Atlanta, Georgia: 38.9%

❀   Myrtle Beach, South Carolina: 36.5%

❀   Fort Collins-Loveland, Colorado: 35.1%

According to the Bureau of Labor Statistics, the following cities ranked the highest in the country in terms of restaurant industry job growth:

Metro Area	Employment	2000 Growth
Las Vegas	53,000	10.6%
Sacramento	46,800	6.6%
Boise	14,700	6.5%
Indianapolis	66,600	6.1%
New Orleans	51,500	6.0%
Memphis	35,400	5.7%
Reno	9,600	5.5%
Dallas	123,300	4.8%
New York City	182,700	4.8%

Austin, TX   46,700   4.7%
But there are some factors to contemplate before assuming the public will rush your doors as soon as you open them, the first and foremost being researching the physical market you'll call home for years to come.

Where Will You Plant Stakes?

I had written once about a pizza shop in California that closed after being open for only two years. Poor product or bad service was responsible for shuttering the place—the owner blamed a lousy location. After his first shop was a success, the owner took the leap and opened his second unit—only to close it two years later, losing $200,000 in the process. But a lesson on effective market research and site selection was learned: afterward he opened three successful units in other Southern California locations.

Market analysts and researchers say the key to finding the perfect location for your shop means to "maximize the potential of the consumer dollar." How do you do that? Simple—you open your doors in the neighborhood of consumers who will eat your pizza. The hard part comes in finding that neighborhood.

I'm not going to sit back and suggest not to spend the money on a reputable market research firm. Such companies are excellent at what focused and detailed information you receive—you want to know how many 18 to 34 year-olds own tarantulas, they'll tell you. But for a price. Information is, after all, valuable. Research firms charge from $100 to well over $100,000, depending on what information is needed and what services are performed.

It's also possible to do some of the market research yourself, at least some preliminary research of a prospective market. Even if you only compile some basic demographic reports, at least that service charge is omitted.

One market researcher once told me that he thought 95 percent of the Ma and Pa restaurant owners open up a store without any thought of a location within a market. I would've taken his comments with a grain of salt if it hadn't been for the fact that he headed up a real estate consultant firm that had analyzed markets for big names like McDonald's, Olive Garden, Pizza Hut and Papa Gino's. He'd seen too many small operators rush too quickly into a new market without looking.

Will your pizza restaurant be successful in a certain market? You'll know if you know who your customers will be. Bertucci's, for instance, has upscale clientele because of its high-end, pricey pizza, and the company's stores are optimally placed in areas that can afford the product—such as areas with $60,000 income or greater. Bertucci's also does about 40 percent takeout, and units often appear near office parks. Domino's has a very inexpensive pizza, and units can easily be placed in markets with incomes of $40,000 to $50,000.

This research results in a customer profile. If you're unsure of who your customer will be in a prospective market, begin first by researching a company selling a similar menu as what you're proposing, and map out where their stores are located. The demographics of customers coming and going is another hint as to who to target as your customer-in-waiting. But it's not good practice to play follow the leader, opening shop where everyone else is—otherwise, if it were an effective strategy, the competition threshold would be too great for practical business.

When poring through a demographic report, you're looking for the key attributes that make up your customer profile, including:

- ❀ Population density
- ❀ Personal income
- ❀ Age groups
- ❀ Ethnic population
- ❀ Employment statistics

Demographic reports can be created with software on your PC, accessed over the Internet, or acquired from a market research firm.

With demographic information in hand, you're ready to scope out a market. Scoping out a market can begin with a simple street map. Laying it out flat, draw the boundaries of the ideal areas, or geographical segments, within the larger market. These segments are your proposed trade areas. Within the trade areas, highlight the following in different colors or notation:

- ▶ Competition
- ▶ Main thoroughfares
- ▶ Direction of traffic flow
- ▶ Other places of interest, such as malls, movie theaters, and other business generators.

Five years ago, acquiring detailed information about markets (both domestic and international) was hard to come by, even for the research pros. But today the resources are a mouse click away, and are much less expensive, if not free. For instance, to find out data on the number of households within a certain diameter from the location you're considering, contact the local post office—there you can find out critical information, like population density.

The important thing to note is that there's knowledge, and then there's wisdom. Wisdom is simply applying the knowledge you've acquired; don't make the mistake of learning all there is to know about an area, only to pass up a golden opportunity, or investing a lot of money on a poor site in a mismatched market.

The Direction of Tomorrow's Pizza Lover

Trends are following the footsteps of aging generations. And the big spenders, those Baby Boomers (82 million people ages 35 to 55) with deeper pockets than any other group—and the largest, outnumbering Generation X and Generation Y combined), are leading the pack. Gearing your concept and product to reach the Boomers and the Echo Boomers close behind will keep you in front of the cash flow.

With the aging population comes a shift from QSR (quick-service restaurant) growth to FSR (full-service restaurant) growth. For the last decade, restaurant growth has been dominated by the QSR segment. The next decade will undoubtedly see the FSRs coming out ahead. Why? Boomers like personal connections with family, friends and associates, and they relish being able to custom order what they eat and drink. This is the "me" generation, remember? Fast food just won't do for them in the years to come, and with healthy levels of disposable income, they can afford to discriminate.

For you, realize that offering limited service may not completely cut you off from sales, but it does ... well, limit you in terms of sales off tomorrow's hungry population groups. Of course, there's no stereotypical tag for the average Boomer—they're as diverse as their tastes. But being open-minded in terms of menu changes, additions, and dining atmosphere will benefit you. Meeting customers' needs, after all, is a large part of running an operation.

Of the big chains, take Pizza Hut parent Tricon as a winner in this area. Not only are they maximizing their real estate dollar, but they're appealing to the increasing diversity among the consuming public by literally putting all their concepts (Pizza Hut, KFC and Taco Bell) under one roof. We'll talk more about this concept later.

You, too, can outline some strategies, such as:

☛ Thinking about what other complementary offerings you can include in your concept

☛ Include extra menu items on your carryout and delivery menus

☛ Mold your environment to your core customers— the younger set likes it bright and free, the older set likes calming and unobtrusive decor, the Boomers like a personal touch and an open floor plans.

When looking at specific markets, keep in mind that many urban areas around the country are revitalizing and revamping. I've been in many cities, such as Charlotte, North Carolina, that are trying to get back in touch with its history. After the banking giants moved into downtown Charlotte and made the city the third largest banking center in the United States, city planners looked around and discovered that downtown didn't have any soul. So now they're spending millions to encourage shopping and nightlife, and it's working. For the pizza entrepreneur, the good side is there's plenty of incentives and tax breaks to open up a downtown eatery.

One thing cities include in their long-term wants

when it comes down to revamping their inner cities is increased foot traffic. And once the foot traffic increases, a pizzeria's business increases.

There's also the growing Latino market in the United States. This is truly an untapped market. The Latino population is growing at a rate six times higher than that of the general population, and currently has a consumer spending power of more than $273 billion. Consider these facts:

☞ The U.S. has the fifth largest Latino population in the world—about 30 million Latinos.

☞ Between 1995 and 2000, U.S. Latinos accounted for roughly 37.5 percent of the total U.S. population growth. By 2005, they'll outnumber African-Americans as America's largest minority group.

☞ Today's youthful Latino population is tomorrow's consumer; their average age is 25, compared to 34 for the general market. This means the market is poised for even more growth.

☞ Zeroing in on the high-concentration areas is easy—more than 70 percent of the U.S. Latino population lives in four states: California, Florida, New York and Texas. More than 45 percent of the population lives in just five cities: Chicago, Los Angeles, Miami, New York and San Francisco.

Getting your name in front of this growing segment of our society will reap immediate and long-term rewards.

Pizza Platitude #1

"An idea can turn to dust or magic, depending on the talent that rubs against it."

Tenet of
Advertising

2

Dynamics of the Biz

In the pizza world, there are two different types of businesses ran by two different types of operator: the independent operator and the chain operator. Never before are the differences more distinct between these two types of pizzeria operator, and never before must these differences be held into account when understanding them. As the chains grow stronger and the competition more fierce with dwindling market shares, many cities are bearing witness to trench warfare, pitting independent operator fist-to-fist with the chain guys. It's in these situations where the differences in business management are most striking.

Many have asked what the definition of both an independent operator and a chain operator is. At Pizza Today, the breakdown of our annual "Hot 100" listing is of companies and independents, the determining factor of an independent being if there are less than 10 stores under one ownership. And for the companies, or chains, we begin with the largest amount of stores (Pizza Hut, of course, being number one), down to the 100th. In this sense, a chain can be defined as any company with more than one store, even though a two-unit operator may be listed under "independent." The important difference to determine is the operator who owns and still has hands-on activity in the day-to-day operation of his pizzeria(s), and the operator who owns shops ran by other people. Typically the independent is the one with sauce on his hands at the end of the night; the chain guy is calling the shots from an office (but I have to be careful here—some chain owners' heads are still in the kitchen, and to take them from the roost beside the ovens is closely related to death).

Obviously, the more stores in a company, the less likely an independent is in the shops mixing it up. This is neither good nor bad—just be aware that there's a different mindset. And just as everyone is different in his or her own way, so to are pizzeria operators. Some one-unit guys are more willing to try new technology than, say, an owner with 20 stores. But knowing where each has come from, and what it is that takes up the bulk of their working day, can greatly benefit relationships and increase the trust factor.

Independent's Day

The independent operator (a.k.a. "indie") possesses a unique outlook on business. Here is a person who has decided to open up his own pizzeria, usually for one reason: for the love of the pie. One compatriot of mine once told me he couldn't help but make pizzas the rest of his life, because he had "sauce in his veins." He had even tried supervising a department at Wal Mart (and was successful at it), but the truth was that his motivation was making and selling pizza. This compulsion to fling dough and make a business of it is undoubtedly the single strongest force that drives the independent, as well as his business mind.

And think about it—given sufficient talent and people skills, success is sure to follow. All the big boys were once independent operations (the Carney brothers with Pizza Hut, Tom Monaghan with Domino's, John Schnatter with Papa John's). It's the love of the pie that drove them from other careers to pursue pizza, and it's on this course that their fates lie. Some, however, don't make it. While impossible to pinpoint the cause of every pizzeria's failure on one cause, many have been shuttered due to bad business decisions usually based on little inside education and false expectations. And it's this bad decision-making that independents strive to avoid.

As opposed to the bigger players (even the 20-unit guy), the single or two-store operator doesn't have a lot of resources to play with, or in some instances, to gamble with. A decision to purchase a new conveyor oven at $12,000, plus installation, will set an indy back much further than a bigger player. Lease options, therefore, are more appealing to the indy than a straight purchase, even for smaller equipment. In a word, indies have more to lose up front with equipment purchases than others, and an equitable write-off schedule with obvious cost benefit is often sought.

Independents take excessive pride in their location, their food, and their reputation. The fact that they're still in existence is kudos enough. A little research reveals what the pizzeria is famous for, or what its unique niche is. Does Joe's Pizza Shack have Sports Night on Thursday nights? Then the operator may very well be a sports fan, using the event as a marketing tool to attract the local high school sports fans and players.

It's also a fact that indies are less likely to break their traditional ways of doing things. There are many reasons for this:

✓ The current operator is the son (or daughter) of the original proprietor, who always did it this way, and therefore defies to break his father's tradition (and possibly fearful of doing so to avoid offending customers who have remained loyal to, say, the thicker pepperoni).

✓ The pizzeria was founded by an Italian family or group, and changing recipes or cooking methods is like spitting blasphemy during mass.

✓ The prevailing attitude among management is: If it ain't broke, don't fix it.

✓ The belief that, when considering back-of-the-house equipment such as mixers, rollers and ovens, over-mechanization can do more harm that good, in terms of injury and taking away the human touch in food preparation.

One clear example is the unwillingness of many indies who have hand-tossed their dough for decades. Trying to sell him a dough sheeter, or a divider/rounder, will prove futile most of the time. His traditional way of forming dough for pizza crust is set in his mind, and telling him there is a better way of doing it may even offend him in a profound way.

Why the dedication to certain ways of doing things, such as hand-forming instead of forming by machine? You'll find out in Chapter Four. You can also learn from talking with a successful indy why he feels one method is better than another.

Takin' It On The Chain

A chain operator is a different animal. First, let's set

apart the chain pizzeria unit manager and his boss. To do this, we must further breakdown the chain on its size and structure of ownership, because approaching a Pizza Hut unit manager is much different than talking shop with the 20-unit operator.

✓ A unit manager for a large chain will undoubtedly refer critical decisions up the chain of command (i.e., when approached about purchasing equipment, changing vendors, new store site selection, etc.).

✓ A unit manager for a smaller chain may also confer with his superior, but the manager has more influence in the decision-making process.

The difference here is a common situation: the smaller chain's upper management often hand picks those individuals who run the individual stores, and opinion is more readily valued with these unit managers. This isn't to say the opinions of store managers are mute with the larger companies. The jest here is that management decisions which make a pointed impact is greater with the small company, due to a shorter chain of command.

One example is the various levels of "buyers" within the chain's hierarchy. Titles range from Acquisitions Director to Vice President of Operations to Vice President of Franchise Operations to Bob, the guy who gets the stuff. Whereas, with an indie or smaller chain, there's only Bob.

Continual Changers

In the world of pizza, as in many other business segments, those companies who seem to always be on the cutting edge of product promotions and menu exclusivity will be the most eager clients. Unique to pizza is the fact that most companies fall into this category. Even the single-unit operator who, on the surface, seems to be content in his age-old operations and simple menu, is brimming with desire for a change or expansion of product or services in his heart of hearts.

Coming out with new promotions, even on a limited basis, lives as an unspoken rule in the back office. Pizza Hut rarely passes six months without a new promotion: the hugely successful Big New Yorker remained Pizza Hut's only new concept for a staggering 18 months, and was finally canonized with the rollout of The Insider. Even during that time, the company re-introduced The Edge.

Companies that have prided themselves in the simplicity of their base menu, shunning introducing new products, have also felt this universal tug for change. Papa John's went head-to-head promotionally with Pizza Hut, rolling out its revamped thin crust at the same time as The Insider. These two products alone required extra smallwares, and, if not already existent in every store worldwide, the purchase of dough forming equipment such as dough sheeters. Of course there were extra boxes needed with the promotional imprints, which meant extra or contracted work for specialty printers and box manufacturers.

Getting the pulse of what companies, great and small, seek in their operations can pay huge dividends for you in the future. By discovering first what his fundamental operation consists of, and then finding out what changes have occurred in the operation over the years. Did Joe of Joe's Pizza Shack jump on the vegetarian pizza bandwagon when pizza lovers went on the health kick? Was Joe prompted to do a chicken line when competitors down the street introduced their new line? When business grew, did

Joe upgrade from a 40-quart mixer to a 60-quart, or did he decide to supplement by going with frozen or parbake doughs?

Talk about such changes in the industry over the years with an operator that's successful—and believe me, successful operators love to talk about success—and you'll see a working image of continual change. Pizza is the most dynamic, thriving, and evolving business I know. It will take someone able to read the signs of the times who can keep the dynamic pace, while thriving, and evolve along with the changes to be a long-lasting success.

Break it Down: Differences of Dine-in, Carryout and Delivery

When speaking of pizzerias, I prefer to call them pizza restaurants. The reason is, yesterday's "pizzeria" is quickly becoming outdated for today's consumer; that is, the little corner shop that serves pizza as its sole offering. The only exception is the landmark shotgun venues in New York City, usually ran by the original founding Italian pizzaiolo or a close relative. These are the pizzerias with a decades-old following, a loyal crowd that ordering elsewhere an act of sacrilege.

But for the other 90 percent of the country, the evolution of the pizza shop is nearing its mature stage—where menus are stuffed to the seams with dozens of pizza types, pasta, sandwiches, appetizers, and so on. We'll talk more about menu strategies to lure and keep a picky consuming public later.

For now, understand that the pizza business is broken down in three segments: dine-in, carryout and delivery.

It's interesting to note how dine-in was king of the ring in terms of what was available some 15 years ago. As the American dining public became more time-squeezed and convenience-oriented, so did pizza to accommodate.

It's no surprise, then, that carryout and delivery are in demand. In 2000, pizza consumers used carryout 42.1 percent of the time (compared to an all-QSR average of 32.6 percent); ordered delivery 36.2 percent of the time (all-QSR average of 8.9 percent); and ate in the restaurant 20.5 percent of the time (all-QSR average of 30.7 percent). Focusing on carryout and delivery procedures will undoubtedly reap bountiful rewards.

Whatever combination of these three segments determines what sort of basic concept you plan to operate. As for one of these segments, one with special issues to consider when implementing and maximizing its operation, as an operator, you either love it or you hate it—delivery. You love it because consumers correlate delivery with pizza and pizza with delivery. Delivering pizza is the quintessential service idea as it ties in with some of the unique aspects of pizza (portability, convenience), and is practically critical in certain areas like college campus locations.

But then, some operators cringe at the thought of introducing delivery into their operation. The reasons include, among others: liability—both the cost of insurance and the remote possibility that an accident may create bad press; cost of operations—it's been estimated that it costs stores $2-$3 per delivery; interruption or distraction of other elements of the business; and finding qualified drivers.

That said, the majority of pizzerias do deliver,

roughly three-quarters of franchised pizza restaurants. You see this on the international front as well, with chains like 320-unit Pizza Pizza in Canada and 760-unit TelePizza in Spain, both the largest players in their respective countries and deriving their business almost totally by delivery.

Some special issues surrounding pizza delivery have surfaced over the years, including whether or not to charge for delivery. The decision to tack on a delivery charge (whether it be 50 cents, $1, $2, whatever) to orders is usually based on an attempt to recoup some of the associated costs—there's always some sort of driver reimbursement on the store's end to act as incentive for driving one's own car (if that's the case) whether a percentage of sales delivered or a per-run pay-out. Those delivering free do so on the basis that pizza is one food delivery concept that's related to an extra arm of service. In fact, pizza delivery began as a free service to entice customers to order the service. Now, as with many things—such as the 30-minute delivery expectation, which Domino's helped to ingrain in the public's mind—it has become expected in many markets.

Another hot topic is redlining, the practice of not delivering in select areas (which are normally in a trade area, or delivery zone) because of high crime. Redlining is fairly common in urban areas, where reports of shootings or other violent crimes are frequent, or drivers have been robbed before. On the store's end, it's simply a matter of keeping drivers out of harm's way. On the consumer's end, if I'm a law-abiding citizen who happens to live in a bad neighborhood, and can't get delivery, there's an issue.

As a result of discrimination suits brought against Domino's recently, the company took a proactive initiative to document the need for redlining a certain zone. Although it seems a bit time consuming for unit managers, it's worth it—reports on crime in certain neighborhoods are gathered from police departments and community business and local government agencies to prove that redlining is necessary for the safety of a store's drivers. If a suit is brought against a store, the documentation is there.

I can't tell you the number of newspaper and wire reports I have stored away that detail violence against drivers. The stacks of clips actually got to a point where I began throwing them away. Sadly, that's the society we live in; I hope what's working for Domino's in their approach to the driver safety and redlining issue will work for everyone.

Delivery can be a real Catch-22 for an operator. One of my drivers was robbed while filling his car up at a gas station. Another had his vehicle pelted with beer bottles and turned upside-down during an out-of-control block party—done while he was at a customer's door making change. Yet, because a good percentage of that unit's sales were from delivery (some of which came from students at Indiana University), and the instances were rare, the service remained open.

Conceptual Variances: Delco, Full-scale and Upscale

These three major service facets determine how you're going to get hot pizza from the oven to the customers' mouths. They also play into what you have in mind for concept development--basically one of three different types of pizza restaurant: the delivery-carryout only (delco) unit, the full-service sized unit, and the upscale unit.

The factors that differentiate each concept are primarily the amount of menu offerings and square footage of operations, as well as what's offered: whether it be dine-in, carryout or delivery, or all three.

A delco offers only carryout and delivery, and is usually found in a strip mall or other location like a convenience store or airport. With many delcos, dough is transported from a commissary or delivered par-baked or frozen due to limited space (fresh dough requires extra prep room to house a mixer and storage racks) in an average 1,200 square feet. Delcos also offer a limited menu, such as pizza, breadsticks and canned soda, with an average guest check of $8.50 or so. There is also no seating, other than a few chairs or benches for waiting carryout customers.

The next step up in terms of square footage, menu complexity and service modes is the full-service unit, like an average-sized Pizza Hut. Usually housed in an average 3,000 square feet, the full-scale operation offers dine-in service (with servers waiting tables), delivery (if so chosen), and carryout. These units show up in strip malls, inside larger malls, or in a freestanding unit with a parking lot. A menu consisting of non-pizza items like wings, garlic bread, beer, fountain soda, sandwiches and salad bar, increases the average guest check to around $11.

For the full-service unit, the most numerous of the three, table turn is key to high volume. The more waiters, waitresses, bussers and dish-washers you have during a lunch or dinner rush, the quicker the turn, which means higher sales. The average full-service pizza restaurant seats 80.

When you get into the upscale pizza restaurant, you're basically looking at an upscale Italian place, or possibly even a restaurant with a Tuscan-American flair, that sells a ton of pizza. There's a full menu with extensive and diverse offerings, and the dining room is dressed up in a traditional Italian motif, even going to extremes like imported Italian lamps or paintings.

A high volume of pizza and entrees is sold via carryout, dine-in or delivery in either a freestanding location with a parking lot, or in a large mall. Seating is usually at 200, but I've seen some behemoths that seat close to 300. Those units were netting around $2.5 million in annual sales, thanks to efficient table turn.

An average guest check of approximately $15 is seen in units that average 5,000 square feet in the upscale arena.

What You'll Pay to Open the Doors

Startup costs for pizza restaurants are based on the concept level (delco, full-service and upscale), due to MEP (mechanical, electrical, plumbing, ventilation), otherwise known as leasehold improvements, and the extra smallwares and equipment needed as you increase in concept size.

It's impossible to arrive at an exact startup cost ahead of time, but you can see on paper what equipment's needed and, given average industry data, what cost per square foot to expect. This will give you a ballpark figure to use in your business plan.

For simplicity's sake, let's assume you're building out in an existing building. For a delco unit, you can plan on spending roughly $40 per square foot—costs go up to around $70 per square foot for an upscale site. A full-service facility falls somewhere in between. Extra plumbing, doors, electrical layouts and other items causes the price to jump so drastically. When you consider extras like the imported paintings, then your price really skyrockets.

Following are some pretty accurate estimates, taken that new equipment is purchased and construction takes place in an existing building, which is leased, and include items like permits and licenses.

A delco's build-out will run approximately $48,000 without equipment figured in; with equipment, $250,000. For a full-service unit, count on $160,000 minus the equipment; $650,000 with. And the upscale will put you back approximately $350,000 with no equipment, and about $750,000. These are the numbers I've seen up til the present, but, of course, if you're leasing equipment or get a great break on rent, costs can be much lower.

Take my advice and seek the advice of the pros. Consult with architects, general restaurant contractors and the many wise consultants in the Resource section of this book. Whether you're gutting an existing shop or building from scratch, it's an arduous and sometimes painful process. Take at least one burden off your back and pay someone else to take the pain!

Fruitful Franchising

If the amount of investment (time as well as money) seems overwhelming, whether you're just starting your prototype unit or you're ready to build your second or third location, there's another option—purchase a franchise. I know, I know, you're thinking: "What, and give up the opportunity to start my own place?" Well, depending on whom you franchise from, the ownership can be just as real. And, your distribution channels are already established, as is possibly decor and marketing strategies.

Franchising is big business. Franchise Recruiters Ltd. conducted a survey of system expansion opinions and executive outlook estimates for development from 100 top-producing franchisors called the Annual Franchise Business Development Survey; it predicted a 13-percent growth for franchising in 2001.

There is one statistic that's a bit troubling, however: One estimate has it that 80 percent of franchise companies fail. Whether this is the fault of franchiser or franchisee, I haven't the slightest. What I do know is that you're able to be prepared with a set of watchful eyes and plenty of questions going into the deal.

The initial pizza franchising boom hit in the late 1950s and into the '60s. Pizza Hut, Domino's and Little Caesars were all founded during those early years and now dominate the industry's franchising with more than 17,800 units.

The bigger the company, the more leverage they hold on their side of the economies of scale, bringing mega-purchasing power, lower food costs, and expeditious systems. This is why franchising is so hot into today, because everybody wants these lopsided benefits. I see more and more 5- to 20-unit operations seeking franchisees to enlarge their territory—good news, really, for the entire industry, due to healthy competition.

A byproduct of this intensely competitive nature is increased levels of product creativity, marketing innovation, and the spawn of non-traditional locations.

As mentioned before, menus are breeding grounds for new items. Chicken wings, stuffed peppers, garlic balls, roasted veggies, white pizza—all are the result of such effort to diversify menus, to stand out from the crowd. This, not only to drive sales, but to attract franchisees. New products are exciting—and why not? It excites consumers, too. Why else would Pizza Hut strive so hard to constantly develop new products—Stuffed Crust, The Insider, The Big New Yorker—when it could probably afford to sit on its haunches a while? Because they know the value of change and diversification.

Even with a limited menu, such as with Papa John's, a new type of pie every so often never hurts. The one area where Papa John's has excelled is in establishing a strong foothold in non-traditional locations, such as sports arenas and airports. Other examples come to mind, such as mama ilardo's and Noble Romans.

Non-traditional locations bring a lot to the table during franchise talks. Opening shop in locations that are high-traffic, while saving space and lowering overhead costs is attractive bait. But perhaps the latest trend in franchised stores is the prospect of opening doors overseas. Talk about non-traditional locations. The big chains have been on foreign land for years, but even smaller players are getting into the international expansion game, like 23-unit Bearno's for one example, which recently sold a franchising agreement to open 40 stores in the next five years in China.

Multi-concepting is another recent franchising trend, where various franchises are owned by one company. It's how players like Boston Pizza and Round Table have infiltrated some areas, selling franchises to other concepts. The company that owns franchises in two or more restaurant chains is able to spread expenses thinner than he would if he only owned a single chain. Although there have been past problems with this corporate setup (Boston

Market is one example, failing system-wide after franchising out to various multi-conceptors), it's still hot in the pizza world: 20 of the 50 leading companies that own multi-concepts own pizza brands. The financial backing of such large companies may be of interest to some.

Whatever attracts a person to a franchise, it should be enough to motivate him to stay on for the long haul. Franchise fees vary greatly, in terms of required up-front capital and profit percentages paid monthly or quarterly. There's as great a variation in franchise agreements, which spell out how much flexibility exists in your own operations. Some franchisors won't look your way unless you're packing enough financially to be able to open ten or more stores in your region. Others are happy you're on board, if only to operate one unit successfully the rest of your life.

When buying a franchise, investigate the franchisor thoroughly. If they're good enough to allow you to succeed under their umbrella, there won't be any problems getting the information you need. And when it comes down actually signing the franchise agreement, be sure you understand what you're reading. Experience pizza people will tell you to land an attorney at this stage, before anything is signed.

But you can get some details up front. Seek specific information, such as finding out if:

1. The franchisor is offering you an exclusive territory, and for how long;

2. You have the first right of refusal to adjacent territories;

3. The company will assist you in locating a spot for the operation;

4. The company provides financing;

5. The franchisor can provide financials—i.e., the last three

years' profits;
6. There are any limitations for menu additions or changes;
7. You are entitled to use any federally trademarked trade names, logos, symbols, etc., without reservation;
8. There is enough time and manpower allocated for training.

Mistakes can be costly when purchasing a franchise. There are some high-end operations that require a minimum $50,000 investment just to get in the door. One I know of doesn't allow the franchisee payback from net profits until the entire build-out cost has been recouped. But the wait is worth it, at least for the stores in operation at the time of this printing—these stores crank out around $40,000 in sales every week. But for such arrangements, if the store doesn't profit, investors may stand to lose a lot of personal wealth and property. I have no doubt that these investors are truly confident they're going to succeed!

There are also costly mistakes that go beyond the initial investment, such as reputation, personal sacrifice, and lawsuits. Many mistakes are made by franchisees by not understanding which party has what responsibilities, as outlined in the disclosure statement. The ball can be dropped easily and without notice when confusion creeps in. UFOCs can be up to 80 pages long. My best advice is to jot down notes as you pore through each section, and get all blurry points clarified up front.

Other big mistakes include: not retaining legal eagles that are ideally experienced in franchising; not contacting a fair amount of current franchisees to see how things "really are"; going in under-capitalized (this goes for everything—pre-opening costs, your own personal budget, opening operating cash, etc.); and going in blind in a market (see previous section).

Here are some statistics from a recent profile from 1,226 companies made available by the International Franchise Association (www.franchise.org):

▶▶ 53% of franchise companies have 50 or fewer total units;

▶ One-third of franchisors studied offered financing;

▶▶ 82% of the companies studied for the profile set royalties as a percentage of sales, and of those, the most common range was 3% to 6%;

▶▶ 72% of franchises charged an advertising fee;

▶▶ Protected territories were offered by 70% of the companies;

▶▶ Area development programs were available among more than a quarter of those studied;

▶▶ Nearly two-thirds of the franchise companies had been in business 12 years or more.

Many reputable pizza franchisors are listed in the Resource section, as are numerous legal resources. I suggest talking with a few of them—if not to get into bed with them, at least to find out what they're about, what their franchising strategy is. You may reach a point down the road when you're on the other end, deciding to franchise your own pizza company.

Let's take a look at the other side of the franchising equation ...

Pop Bible Quiz: What was the first thing God said to Adam? No, it wasn't "So, what do ya think of Eve?" It was "Be fruitful and multiply." The same goes for you, the pizza professional, if you're eyeing expansion either now or in the future.

Fruitful franchising—when franchising is in its

busiest season and people rush to buy the next one—occurs during economic downturns. The reverse is true for times of prosperity, when CEO Chuck is content in his current high-paying position at Big Name, Inc. Turn down the financial faucet to a trickle, and Chuck's seeking a new venture.

On the other end, when—and if—you decide to franchise your baby out, how do you find acceptable franchisees? Bear in mind that you're up against a lot of competition. The International Franchise Association (IFA) reports that 76 pizza-concept companies were selling franchises in 1993, and increased to 97 five years later where it stayed through 2000.

Getting bigger store-wise may not be your destiny. I recall one operator in Ohio who related his frustration when comparing himself with other fast-growing pizza companies. He had begun his operation the same year Domino's had, and 20 years later he remained in his one store. He began wondering what he was doing wrong. The solution came in the form of a consultant, who offered some sage advice: look at what you have—a successful, money-making restaurant, a genuine landmark in small town USA. Think of what you may end up with if you aggressively expand—a couple of stores that lose money, a couple that make money, and a whole other set of headaches. The operator has since opened two other locations near his original unit, and is content with what he has.

In fact, digging beneath the surface, I discovered that he really hated to part with his recipes, handing them over to franchisees. There was a very real fear that his recipes would be stolen and used to make pizza, pasta, sauce and bread in another person's restaurant. Limited control is what he really desired, not immense expansion.

He probably wouldn't get a good night's sleep if he had grown like Domino's.

When, and if, you do franchise, it's a good idea to communicate your vision with potential franchisees before anyone signs anything. It's in your best interest, especially when first franchising your concept, to have one-on-one meetings with potential franchisees.

Jim Fox, president of Fox's Pizza Den out of Pittsburgh, told me once how he introduces franchise suitors to his way of business life. In an effort to expose them to what Fox has to offer, he puts them up overnight near his corporate offices, and they're taken from one store after another.

Product is sampled, and Fox has a chance to get his point across—what his company is all about. As he told me: "We make sure they really like it before they become too involved with it." Fox's approach has resulted in a stable of 219 open units, with 18 more planned to open this year.

From my interaction with operators over the years, this personal method ends with better results on both ends, as opposed to commissioning franchise brokers. These brokers may charge big fees for their work and can lead to partnering up with new franchisees that marry well with your concept or working philosophy.

As you grow, it's smart to create a tenured franchise staff of your own to handle the details (i.e., real estate, other property acquisition, etc.).

Lawyers play a big role, too, as they prepare franchise documents and contracts. Don't try handling these yourself—the forms must follow hard-and-fast regulations overseen by the Federal Trade Commission and some local governments.

Placing ads in local newspapers and sending direct mail to prospects is an affordable way of advertising your franchising company. But as with any other sales program, hot leads are like gold. Hot leads often originate from competitors or existing franchisees. As with your best form of advertising, if you're doing the right thing all along, word-of-mouth advertising will bring them to you.

There's a very informative newsletter called FranchiseHelp Online, created by Mary Tomzack, the author of a great guide titled Tips & Traps When Buying a Franchise. As much as my own e-newsletter *Pie Times* centers on the pizza industry, *FranchiseHelp* Online gives a synopsis of current issues and opportunities. You can check it out at www.franchisehelp.com. The company is a good source, too, for selection, evaluation and rating of domestic and international franchise opportunities, as well as assisting independents looking to franchise their concept. They also sell the franchising world's list of lists, Uniform Franchise Offering Circulars (UFOCs).

Pizza Platitude #2

Pleasure in the job puts perfection in the work.
Aristotle (384BC - 322BC) Greek writer, philosopher

3

Menu Evolution

The evolution of menus found in pizza restaurants isn't just a theory—it's fact. As transportation and communication acted to shrink our world and our borders, culinary idiosyncrasies blurred from one culture to another and we now have the varied palate of the adoring public. No doubt customer requests for one obscure topping or another has developed into specialty combination pies that stayed on menus for years, or have even contributed to shops' specialty reputations.

Understanding where customers' preferences come from (and where they may still evolve) will allow you to arrange a menu with choice offerings.

First, some generalizations about the various pizza styles in our country. Then we'll dive into the particulars that will make your menu sing.

There are three major regional styles of pizza in the United States. In the East, pizza is the traditional Neapolitan type with a light, thin crust, tomato sauce, mozzarella cheese and a vegetable or meat topping. It's more commonly known as New York-style, a type of pie with the deepest history dating back to the turn of 1900.

Gennaro Lombardi opened the first American pizzeria in 1905 in New York City (Lombardi's), the pizza from which came a product of his Neapolitan upbringing—a thin-crust pie that was identical to that found in his hometown. Identical, save the cheese: true Neapolitan pizza was topped with mozzarella di buffala (using milk from water buffalo), whereas Lombardi used mozzarella derived from cow's milk. The dough he used, and what is considered to be the only type to use if you want to call your pizza "New York style", is a high-gluten, hard spring wheat flour that's considerably wet (some say a moisture content of at least 55 percent).

New York style pizza dough is always hand-formed—hardliners say that using anything mechanical spoils the authenticity, even a rolling pin! The reason behind this is because this type of crust must bake with a puffy outer rim, and mechanical forming will press the lip out flat, as well as produce a near perfectly round shape. New Yorkers expect their pies to be obviously hand-formed, distorted a bit, never perfectly round. Other specifics include fresh mozzarella that's either cubed or sliced (never shredded), and sauced with crushed tomatoes—not really sauce at all!

These pies are traditionally cooked in coal-fired ovens, but with dwindling numbers of these ovens in operation you'll find wood-burning and gas-fired decks doing the job. I've even seen some operations running their product through conveyors which have been calibrated just so to give the characteristic "very well done" bottom. New York-style pizza differs from any other pizza in that it's cooked quickly at very high temperatures to give an almost burnt appearance to the bottom side of the crust.

Selling by the slice is also popular with this category. The publisher of *Pizza Today*, Pete Lachapelle, is a native New Yorker, and he'll always make his point that pizza cut in squares isn't pizza at all. To him, and the rest of his confident breed—all 10 million plus—a real pizza experience means picking up a slice, folding it, and eating it as grease and sauce run down your forearm!

Stephen Duncombe, managing partner for Fuel Pizza Cafe in Charlotte, North Carolina, came from his native Manhattan to begin the Fuel chain. He told me that when they began selling pizza by the slice, the Charlotte public would buy a slice—but they didn't know what to do with it. On the east coast, pizza by the slice on the street is akin to hot dogs at a baseball game—it's expected.

On the West Coast, pizza takes on a sophisticated look. Individual-size pizzas with light chewy crust and toppings ranging from sun-dried tomatoes to asparagus to boccocini cheese are the norm. Gourmet pizzas are thought to have been birthed in the San Francisco area back in the '80s; we've seen the rise of California Pizza Kitchen with its unique pizza-making methods and combinations (even breaching the frozen pizza/grocery barrier with them). The light crust complements the region's taste for healthier foods, and ranges in thickness from a very thin-and-crispy to a "middle of the road" traditional or hand-tossed consistency.

Thin-and-crispy differs from New York-style in that the dough is drier, to the point of being crumbly in some stores before proofing (rising), at room temperature for a short time or retarding under refrigeration for a longer period. This type of crust has been tagged by some as an "original California-style". Most pizzerias utilize mechanical forming to roll a thin crust out into a cooking pan by way of using a sheeter or dough roller, and then docked with a spiked roller. Docking prevents larger air bubbles (the dough's cells) from forming during baking.

The Midwestern states prefer the deep-dish style, a thick creation heaped with toppings—some creations are topped so high it requires up to 45 minutes to bake. Chicago, in particular, is home of both the deep dish and the stuffed pizza.

Ike Seawell is widely credited for coming up with the deep-dish pizza in 1943—some call it Chicago pizza or Chicago-style pizza. Using a deep (1 _- to 3-inch wall) pan, a thick crust is made that has a moisture content in the 60- to 65-percent range—quite a wet dough. The dough is normally sheeted to about _ inch or thicker, placed in the oiled pan and proofed in a heating cabinet (proofer) or for a longer time at room temperature. The longer the dough proofs, of course, the thicker the crust. Pizza Hut's version, their Pan Pizza, remains their number-one seller.

In America, stuffed pizza originated some 30 years ago by Joe Boglio, the owner of the Giordano's shops at the time. Stuffed pizza is a pie that's assembled in the following fashion: the bottom crust is laid in a deep pan; toppings are piled on, usually including cheese; a top crust is layered on and crimped together on the edges with the bottom crust; and sauce is applied, sometimes accompanied with cheese. That's the American version anyway; in Italy, where stuffed pizza has been around a while, there is no top sauce.

With these regional preferences in mind, you should be better prepared to conceive a menu that's attractive to the majority of palates in your area. This doesn't mean that you'll never offer a thin-and-crispy crust in Michigan, or a deep-dish pie in Boston. As you'll see in many other aspects, variety is the catalyst of profits when it comes to menus.

From Simple Sausage to Complex Calamari

A lot has changed on America's pizza menu over the course of the years. Alongside the ultra-traditional Margherita Pizza (still on menus today) there's the Seafood Special, with shrimp, tuna, and practically anything that used to swim or crawl on the bottom of one sea or another. You've got goat cheese and capers, gouda and pineapple, even strawberry and peanut butter. Yes, the founding fathers of traditional pizza would look on in wonder if they saw what graces the tables of America in 2001.

Pizza offers the flexibility of such creativity, allowing just about any food to bake well within the confines of its crust, and this allows you, the operator, to profit even more so. Any culinary idea that pops into your head can be combined with a marketing plan, and experimentation can commence right off. Not only with topping combinations, but with the dough itself. Look no further than Pizza Hut's newest pizza, The Twisted Crust. Baking a combo pizza-breadstick creation is a great example of how far a menu can be stretched to attract new customers and fill the void we new-item addicts crave.

In fact, The Twisted Crust isn't anything new in the world of pizza—operators have brainstormed and forced pizza dough's evolution from the ages-old thin crust to deep dish pan pizza and everything in between. It's this accepted, and oftentimes anticipated, variation in toppings and crusts that will dictate in part how successful your menu is.

Take the sampling I just returned from (yes, even as

I write, my taste buds are still relishing the pizzas I was priv-ileged to nibble on). Twenty-plus different contest entries, all unique and well-thought-out pizzas for the Best of the Midwest pizza contest. Only one in each category (seafood, traditional, exotic and winged) will make the finals in Chicago at the Pizza Expo's Pizza Festiva. Good thing I was-n't judging this time around—it would have been difficult to choose a winner!

I tried a pie with coconut, one with artichoke and cream cheese, one that had guacamole and sour cream doppled on, another with a barbeque sauce made from scratch (packed brown sugar, molasses, and stout beer), and yet another topped with grilled calamari. Last year I tried a pizza with bison meat (excellent, by the way). This is what I'm talking about when I say evolving menus.

But regardless of what ingredients are used and made to perfection, the important menu move is focusing on preparation and presentation, with your dough and your toppings. After all, having a handsome menu is one thing; it's quite another to walk the talk, to pull through with what you're advertising.

Remember that eye appeal is buy appeal. A great pizza is one that offers an ideal balance of texture (bite) and flavor that blends every element, from the garnish through the toppings down to the finishing nibble of crust. This takes a commitment to consistency. As an example of stan-dards you can communicate to your kitchen crew for every pizza, take consider these guidelines:

↦   Evenly raised borders: no peaks or valleys or bowl-shaped edges.

↦   Sauce within a certain distance from the pan, creating a border.

↦ Distribute toppings evenly, without any topingredients ending up on the crust (granted you're *wanting* an obvious border—some operators prefer toppings to the edge).

↦ Top with correct portions with measuring cups or other measuring devices (more on this in Chapter 8).

↦ Cut all slices equally and place them together, touching; cut the crust completely through the edge, from the center.

↦ Check for no bubbles.

↦ Check for top doneness, that all the items are fully cooked, but no burned vegetables.

↦ Check that the crust is an even, golden brown on top and bottom, without being splotchy or burnt.

Obviously, this is just a sample of a checklist to make out when checking for product quality and consistency. Yours will be made out according to your specific visual appeal goals of the end product.

Laying Out Your Profits

Your menu is your primary sales vessel. If you doubt that fact, pick out the highest selling item you offer and check to see how it's positioned and featured on the menu. There's an outstanding chance that it's either positioned well or featured favorably with accompanying art or descriptive text. On the other hand, those items that are low-sellers are probably in the shadows of other dishes, or is cursed with a bad caption or outdated art.

Because it's possible to control how well an item sells, you're able to use a menu to exercise some control over what items are placed where, and therefore control food costs. Take that high-cost gouda cheese appetizer—how about putting it in the middle of the section, as opposed to the top. Or that barbeque sandwich that you want to slowly ease off the menu—place it in the middle of the back page. You get the idea.

While this book won't cover all there is to know about menu engineering, do know that it's integral to your pizza prosperity. Get some of the basics down, and you'll at least know some underlying reasons behind why some items move better than others, and have an educated direction when laying out menus of the future.

First off, the menu's overall physical appearance should reflect your brand and service environment. Check to ensure that the menu's paper, printing, color mix, etc. coordinates well with who you are. Customers expect a certain feel and look to a menu based on previous visits and experiences. This goes for past times at your facility as well as other pizza or Italian restaurants that they consider comparable to you in price and offerings. In other words, avoid costly menus if you're a value-driven delco; and conversely, avoid the "bargain" paper stock and printer if you're higher-end.

Physical arrangement of items is one of the most significant menu-making elements. American diners read a menu the same way they read a book or newspaper; that is, from beginning to end, top to bottom, and from left to right. Those items you place first, at the top of a list, will be noticed first and obviously make the greatest impression.

Scientific tests have plotted the patterns of eye movement of menu readers. When a person reads a menu, her eyes scan in the following order, (1) being the first place she looks and (7) being the last:

3		2
	7 1	5
4		6

   If you wish to draw attention to a particular item, another way to catch the eye is by featuring it in a larger type, bold type, or a different font or typeface than the surrounding dishes. Other methods include boxing an item in, separating it from the other items, giving it its own space on the menu, as well as using color photographs and other artwork. The extra cost associated with printing menus that are rich in graphics is invariably paid for soon by increased sales. We live in a graphic-rich and quick read society—think of those TV commercials or print ads that capture our attention. Do the same with your menu.

Varily, Varily

   Oops, sorry. I'm thinking "varied" here in this section.
   Variety on a menu is critical if you want maximum appeal to the public. Variety in food, cooking methods of the food, drinks, and prices. Your intention as the successful pizza restaurateur is to be a draw for the largest possible audience, thereby relying on a broad demographic of pizza lover. This relates to varied crust types, a good mix of veggie and meat toppings, exotic toppings if you're able—it's

handy to have a salad bar, as the ease of use of salad ingredients turns regular pizza into something special (broccoli, asparagus, artichoke hearts, fruit all come to mind).

Some consultants specializing in menu design have said that a minimum of five entrees is the accepted amount for any restaurant menu, and for pizza stores they should include at least one dish each composed mainly of meat, vegetable, fish, and poultry. Throw in cheese (such as for your appetizer section: mozzarella sticks) and you've pretty much built the nutritional pyramid with all the food groups represented.

In terms of various cooking methods, feature dishes that are sauteed, roasted, oven-baked, etc., and make sure customers can read about it in the description. If you house a wood-burning oven, exploit the fact that the public loves to hear about how their peppers are "roasted slowly in our wood-burning oven".

Also consider presentation when laying out your menu and creating combinations. Some food items work better than others in terms of how they look next to each other. The great thing about food is that there's an infinity of combinations you're able to arrange on a plate. Pick and choose what colors contrast interestingly, and what ones don't. Also keep in mind, texture, contour and aroma. Much has to do with experimentation, but the end result is a well-planned menu that's a boon for sales.

Varied prices should be present, keeping the customer in mind who can't necessarily fork out the money for your more expensive items. Again, you're appealing to a wide customer base, not just the middle-upper class—and, conversely, not just the college kids. Even if you're doing business on the edge of a college campus, vary the prices with a few higher-priced items and see who may just go for the gourmet line. Not every college kid is broke, after all, and there are year-round natives in every college town.

Your menu's variety is geared to keep customers coming back for more, so give them what they expect. Every pizza restaurant is dependent on repeat business. Keep your menu up-to-date, fresh-looking, and interesting, and with a broad appeal.

Great menus begin by:

1. Picking the categories you know you'll eventually serve;
2. List all the items that will be offered in each category;
3. Include variety, accurate grammar/composition, and balance;
4. Add descriptive language intended to sell the items;
5. Add art elements and arrange logically;

Get Descriptive

Before customers order, their minds are already racing, their mouths already tasting the food. They're scanning the menu, deciding what's for dinner. This is true not just of dine-in customers, but those delivery patrons glancing over your menu hanging from a magnet from their fridge.

How you describe your product can affect what customers order. Words are powerful—believe me, I know; I'm in the word business. In fact, a description can make someone hungry, just as an ad on TV can. A product's description is a short, quick snapshot of the item, an answer for the reader and a reason to order.

On the other side of the coin, a poorly written description can deter sales. If someone thumbs down to the

Pepperoni King Pizza, and reads "The most pepperoni we can fit on a pizza", he may stumble through it as he tried to determine just how much pepperoni that actually is. But if the pizza is described as "Piled high with 75 slices of thick pepperoni", the order's on the way.

Using appealing adjectives and phrases tends to extract a positive reaction from consumers, and can act to increase guest check averages as well. Upselling begins on the menu, when pitchers of soft drinks are "Only 65 cents more, free refills", as opposed to smaller sizes. Or bundling pizzas with appetizers or drinks "feeds the family for only $4 more!"

Positive, appealing descriptive words and phrases act subliminally. When a customer makes a decision, the item is already perceived as "Gainesville's Best Pizza" or "topped high with fresh mozzarella". The perceived value or quality has been birthed, and the experience is on the way to becoming a wonderful one. So pick your words wisely, get input from others, and before anything else, note how you react to it. Does the description make you hungry?

Stumped with how to say it? Here's some hot terminology for catchy menus:

Abundant	Accented	Additional	Adorned
Alternative	Ample	Appeal	Array
Attractive	Authentic	Awesome	Best
Blooming	Bountiful	Brilliant	Carefully
Choice	Classic	Colorful	Crisp
Delicious	Delectable	Deluxe	Enhanced
Essence	Excellent	Exciting	Extra
Famous	Favorite	Featuring	Festive
Flavorful	Fresh	Garden	Generous

Genuine	Golden	Grilled	Healthful
Hearty	Herbed	Highest	Hot
Impressive	Incredible	Magnifico	Morsels
Mouth-watering	New	Notable	Nourishing
Open-faced	Perfect	Pleasing	Plentiful
Popular	Quality	Refreshing	Sauteed
Savory	Select	Sizzling	Skillfully
Stuffed	Sumptuous	Superb	Superior
Tantalizing	Tasty	Tempting	Tender
Toasted	Tremendous	Ultimate	Unique
Unparalleled	Unprecedented	Utmost	Variety
Vine-ripened	Warm	Whole	Wonderful

It is possible to conceive, construct and create your menu on your own. But I suggest hiring out the job past the conception phase. Ask for references for menu consultants, design companies and branding professionals from your state restaurant association. Or if you particularly like the image and presentation of a menu of another restaurant—yes, even competitors—investigate who they hired for the job.

A reputable menu consultant will charge you around $3,500 to $6,500 for a complete menu engineering job—evaluation, design and layout, printing and materials. Sound pricey? Consider that a super menu can pump sales up to five percent or more, and that right off the bat. Remember that your menu is the one marketing piece that every person interested in your food is going to read!

Cater to Kids, Too!

Let's not leave kids menus out of the discussion. Why a kids menu? One marketing guru told me once that youngsters between 4 and 12 years old will influence the spending of more than $500 billion this year. And the National Restaurant Association reported that families with children constitute 40 percent of spending on food away from home.

Plus, you don't want to be left out of this marketing fray: nine out of 10 under-$15-guest-check restaurants have kid-sized portions at lower prices.

In your kids section of the menu, big selling items include: chicken tenders or chicken fingers; fries; personal-size pizzas (usually pepperoni or plain cheese); spaghetti; ravioli; and buttered pasta. Cookies are always a solid bet to include with a kids meal selection, as are extras like crayons or balloons. Games are also sure to please.

Activity books are also good to have on hand to go along with serving any kids, regardless if they order a kids meal or not. These books can be purchased at low prices, but be sure to incorporate "cool" graphics. In the virtual entertainment world, kids expect full-color excitement, and probably won't be clamoring to come back if you can only offer boring black-and-white books. Of course, place mats that are kid-friendly is another bonus, as it can not only display the kids menu but give them something to do while they wait on dinner.

Cases for Fresh and Pre-prepped

In terms of how you, the operator, receive food before it becomes ingredients on a pizza, there are a few choices. The choices involve how food is packaged and stored, and eventually presented to the customer. You'll make your choice by working backwards from the customer's table: what product do you wish to present, fresh or pre-prepped?

Saying 'fresh', I'm talking about food that is prepared, for use as ingredients, in the restaurant. A more proper term may be 'freshly prepped' food. The reason I bring up this distinction is because pre-prepped/pre-packaged food can be as tasty and as fresh as that which is sliced and diced inhouse.

The flagrant benefits to using freshly prepped product on not only your pizza, but on the salad bar, sandwiches, pasta, etc., are numerous. Discriminating tastes claim they can tell the difference—and that may very well be true—and you're able to market your dishes in that vein. Shops that make their own pasta from scratch exploit that fact on their menus and much of their advertising. I visited one place that paid two employees to hand-roll meatballs eight hours a day. The result: orders for spaghetti and meatballs almost eclipse pizza orders every week!

Pre-prepped/pre-packaged food, on the other hand, has come a long way in just the last five years or so. I remember developing a ritual of writing out return orders for sliced and diced onions and green peppers each week due to faulty seals on the vacuum packs. And I'm sure it's still not unusual for that to occur—it's not an exact science, after all—but back then, the taste simply disappeared after a day or so on the makeline. Some customers commented on the lack of flavor on a variety of our pies due to ingredients' lack of freshness.

Vacuum-sealed packaging has improved a lot, however, and product is staying fresher longer—with the help of preservatives as well. Fresh-product purists will say: "Including preservatives is exactly the opposite of fresh!"

Pre-prepped purists will tell you: "Most people can't taste the difference. Besides, how much do you pay your prep cooks to slice, dice and julienne?"

Labor savings and product consistency are the two benefits that sell many operators. Labor costs savings is especially important in these labor-strapped times, not only because of the ever-present eye on labor costs, but because the majority of pizzeria workers are high-schoolers who aren't able to work prep machinery such as powered slicers. In fact, pre-prepped ingredients makes powered slicers and other equipment either less needed or obsolete, thus drastically reducing overall machine maintenance and even new equipment purchases.

Product consistency wins over when you're still considering your workforce. Turnover in American pizza shops hovers around an average 100 percent, and the constant influx of new workers almost guarantees some inconsistency. Using pre-prepped ingredients rids the shop owner of the nagging concern that the green pepper with a standard _-inch cut will be cut _ inch tomorrow and _ inch the next day. Controlling food costs by using these ingredients is something most managers can put their arms around.

Real world, though, sees shops utilizing both fresh and pre-prepped ingredients. In terms of making fresh pasta, a store may consider that too time-consuming and arduous, yet ship in frozen meatballs. A manager may deem pre-prepped/pre-packaged roasted red peppers too expensive, but takes pride in his hand-sliced pepperoni. As with anything and everything to do with food and the menu it's listed on, the choice depends on the product mix and the individual operator.

One more note on pre-packaged foods: it's not just

vacuum-sealing that ensures freshness during shipping. Vacuum-packing involves drawing all the air out of the plastic packaging just after the product is prepared. This creates more space for efficient shipping, and also increases the shelf life during storage.

Another technology I've seen is 'pillow packing', which allows air to stay inside the package. The pocket of air surrounding the product cushions the food, preventing bruising or other damage during shipping. Contrary to popular belief, the presence of air doesn't cause product to begin the spoilage process—it's the movement of air that's the culprit.

A Chunk of Cheese Knowledge

A discussion on cheese is a book in and of itself. So we'll go light here, and focus in on the latest trends and how cheese is being used in pizza restaurants.

One of the big criteria for judging prize pies during the ongoing Pizza Festiva's Pizza Across America recipe competition is how well the cheese melds with the rest of the pizza. The competition is, after all, co-sponsored by the Wisconsin Milk Marketing Board; but, no, judges aren't executive cheese-heads from any cheese organization. You'll find cheese held as a top priority in any pizza competition around the world—even in Italy, where they always go very light on cheese topping.

Mozzarella is, of course, the primary type used on pizza. But there's variation even with it. Any pizza pro should know the following:

☆ Fresh mozzarella, made from scratch, has a smooth bite and tastes milkier than processed. Although it only has a 24- to 72-hour shelf life, most pizza makers who make their own fresh mozz won't freeze it for fear of destroying its unique consistency and melting qualities.

☆ Part-skim mozzarella is derived from skim milk, has a high water concentration, and has the benefit of drastically reducing the fat content of pizza. Some operators highlight this low-fat fact by advertising their pies as healthy alternatives.

☆ Whole-milk mozzarella is derived from—you guessed it—whole milk, with less water, therefore browning slower. Whole-milk mozz also tends to turn more golden than brown as it melts, and retains a more tender bit over time compared to part-skim.

Some pizza makers still slice, shred and cube their own cheese, but the majority buy from vendors. Because cheese is the one ingredient that is common to all pizza (there are some no-cheese pizzas on menus), it makes sense that to differentiate oneself from the competition you must use your cheese wisely.

This leads to cheese-blending, something that's been around for a long time, yet a technique many think still remains underutilized. As the world shrinks, and cultures introduce other cultures' dishes and tastes, we're seeing more international flavors popping up in cheese blends. So proliferate is the demand for unique blends, some vendors offer to shred or dice almost any combination of cheese, package it and send it out. Today we're seeing a multitude of blends of cheeses like cheddar, Muenster, Gouda, feta, provolone, hot pepper Jack, Parmesan, Romano, Asiago, fontina, and the list goes on.

Blending cheeses is certainly a selling point, and not just for independent operators with creative whims. Pizza

Hut rolled out its Ultimate Cheese Pizza with six different cheeses, and Domino's offered a chicken pizza last year with mozzarella, Romano and Parmesan.

These pies aren't cheap to make, but they are easy to sell. Remember our earlier discussion about how our taste buds love fat? Well, cheese is loaded with it, some varieties more so than others. And the hungry public knows what it likes!

Pizza Platitude #3

*Perfection, fortunately, is not
the only alternative to mediocrity.
A more sensible alternative is excellence.
Striving for excellence is stimulating
and rewarding; striving for perfection—
in practically anything—is both neurotic and
futile.*

Edwin Bliss

4

The Dough Dimension

A pizza's dough is to the finished pie what a foundation is to a house. Think of a well-conceived dough recipe and attentive prep as the sturdy dough that will showcase a top-notch pie. As the Gospels preach, such a house is going to hold up under the storm of high-temperature ovens, being cut apart, and transported to either a table or a house. But the pizza that's built on poorly planned dough formulation and haphazard production will undoubtedly miss the mark customers set for today's quality pie.

To the finished pizza, if a dough is sub-standard, you're apt to see undone spots (or "gummy" areas where the dough hasn't cooked adequately), crashing—much like a poorly prepared cake batter falling during baking, or a whole slew of other nasty problems.

Properly prepared dough, on the other hand, will be like your spouse—you may not give it the love it deserves all the time, but it always makes you look good no matter what. Barring anything out of the ordinary, of course. Pizza dough can only withstand so much handling after all.

How do you prepare dough properly? Well, that all depends on the nature of the dough—is it fresh, frozen or par-baked? Clearly, fresh (from scratch) dough has the most room for error because of the increased handling. Remember that to err is human. And with many human hands involved in various production steps with fresh dough, to be human is to err.

But there are ample opportunities for frozen and par-baked dough to be monkeyed with as well. In the end, no matter what the dough type you're using, you must preach the gospel of using only quality dough. Much too often, operators slide into the rut of using every last possible scrap of dough, even if it means using a cracked frozen dough puck, or an expired par-baked shell, or an over-proofed deep-dish that's sticking to the lid.

Think long-term when you're tempted next to let a late night sub-standard order slide by—those same customers may be the next day's lunch customers. Unless the experience is bad, of course.

Fresh, Frozen and Fully Par-baked

As opposed to the other types of dough (frozen, par-baked, mixed from a pre-packaged dough mix), making dough from scratch is quintessential mom-and-pop handmade freshness. A scratch-made crust is an operator's stamp, one that has no twin. Many operators who continue making their dough from scratch like to be in total control of how their dough tastes and behaves. Plus, for purposes of this chapter, it allows me to explain a pizza crust's ingredients, since it's the ingredients, mixed just right, that turns into the pride of thousands of pizzaiolos.

The main ingredients to any pizza dough recipe is flour, yeast, salt and water. Other ingredients, which aren't necessary for a basic dough but widely used, are oil and sugar. We'll get into other additives and enhancements a bit later.

First, the flour. I'm not going to forage into the details of hard and soft, winter and spring wheats simply for the sake of space conservation, but I do suggest you learn more about these details. General Mills and SAF host a very informative seminar at most every Pizza Expo called the Pizza Crust Boot Camp. Either attend these things and ask questions, or call these people up and get more information (contact names and numbers are in the Resource Section)—you won't regret it.

For our purposes, understand that there are four basic types of flour, each with specific protein ranges (pay attention, you'll be quizzed later):

- ❂ All-purpose flour 10 to 12 percent protein
- ❂ Bread flour   12 to 13 percent
- ❂ High-gluten flour 13 to 14 percent
- ❂ Whole wheat flour 13 to 15 percent

These protein percentages may vary by a half percent or so, but this is a good, general guide. The reason these levels are important is because of how you want your crust to "hold up" or perform after it's mixed and ready to top and bake. Here's a general rule of thumb for choosing which type of flour to use:

- ❂ Use all-purpose flour for deep-dish pizzas
- ❂ Bread flour is a good all-around flour, used by most pizza makers for a medium to thick crust
- ❂ Use a high-gluten flour for thin-crust pies and hand-tossed, or medium-crust pies

The protein level of flour determines the sturdiness and durability of your dough, which in turn determine the "bite" characteristics of your crust. For instance, an all-purpose flour results in a crust that's tender to the bite, less pliable to shape during prep; a high-gluten flour is very tolerant to mixing and shaping, and has a crispy, but often chewy, bite; bread flour is more tolerant during prep handling than all-purpose, but has a softer bite than high-gluten.

In fact, bread flour is widely used because it can be manipulated to create thick and thin crusts, and most anything in between. The difference is found in adjusting ingredients and the amount of ingredients.

Many in the industry prefer using a "hard-wheat" flour that's high in protein, at the 13 to 14-percent level. Such flour maximizes moisture retention during conditioning, a critical factor of preventing drying out while holding for a time, like overnight in a cooler.

Water is the staff of dough life. It hydrates the other ingredients (except oil, of course), and it combines gluten-forming proteins to actually form the sticky mass we recognize as dough—water literally brings life to dough!

A softer dough has more water than a stiffer dough, and therefore you'll see a wide range of water in dough formulations. Water also plays a role in the internal temperature of your dough, which acts as either a catalyst or a stunt for yeast activity. Dough pros have told me in the past to keep a close eye on your water's temperature as well. A good rule of thumb is:

✪ Let your water drop to 38 degrees, and kiss your yeast good-bye;

✪ Drop to less than 70 degrees and you'll get slow yeast reaction;

✪ Get to above 105 degrees and expect an accelerated reaction;

❂ Stay at 75 to 105 degrees and your yeast will act like it should.

Yeast leavens the dough as CO_2 is produced, causing the dough to rise. It's really chemical warfare inside a glob of dough; the CO_2 is produced as yeast gobbles up whatever sugars it can find—this process is called fermentation. (Yes, the same fermentation that's found in some moonshine production—that's why a batch of dough that's overstayed its visit in your shop will begin smelling like you did after an all-night party back in your college days!)

As yeast is a living organism, actively working away inside the dough producing acids and heat which soften the gluten structure, it requires a nurturing environment to do its magic. Too cool of an environment and it lays low, slowing down. Too hot, and it expires, much like we do on a hot summer day after doing yard work. Yeast is the ingredient in dough that produces flavor and aroma and conditions the dough for shaping, and eventually baking like a champion.

There are three different types of yeast including instant dry, compressed and active dry. Any type will work with your dough, and produce similar results, but I've had great success with compressed yeast. Others like using active dry yeast because it's easier to use—it dissolves faster and stores longer. Pro-active dry users also suggest that it distributes easier throughout the dough. Some suggest to treat yeast ideally by re-hydrating it in warm water and then adding it to the dough mix. I've done it both ways, and, again, have had very similar results.

Salt is, well, salt. It enhances flavor, as in most foods it comes into contact with, but it also holds a few pizza dough-specific uses. Salt also enhances the strength of gluten during the dough-making process, resulting in a firmer dough. And, if 1 to 2 percent is used in the formulation, salt will even slow down the rate of fermentation.

But if you want to speed up fermentation, add a little bit more sugar. Even without adding sugar, yeast will actively seek and eat the sugars found naturally in the flour. But toss a bit of sugar in the batch and look out—the yeast will devour it like a turkey on Thanksgiving. This extra work to eat the sugar means more heat produced by the yeast, which means faster fermentation. But don't overdo it. Go up to about 5 percent with sugar; anything over will begin to actually slow it back down.

Oil acts as a lubricant, and I can't name one person who doesn't use some form of it in their dough. As the dough mixes, oil helps to evenly distribute the various ingredients, as well as increasing the extensibility (or, workability during shaping and handling without ripping or tearing). Oil also helps to form a critical barrier between the dough and the sauce that will be applied eventually.

Oil can also act as a barrier in a bad way. Consider the optimal order of dough ingredient mixing: It's best to mix all of them except for the oil, and then add the oil after initially mixing. Follow this sequence: Mix the flour, water, salt, yeast and sugar, for about two minutes at low speed. Once all of the dry flour has been incorporated into the dough, stop the mixer, add your oil and continue mixing for another minute or so on that low speed. Then switch your mixer to medium speed and mix until your heart's content.

The reason the order of ingredient inclusion is important (specifically, oil exclusion until the dough has begun mixing) is an absorption issue. If you throw all your ingredients in together with the oil, the oil will tend to interfere with the water and flour integration. The flour must absorb the water for consistent results, and since oil and water don't mix, the oil can act as a sporadic barrier throughout the dough.

When developing a dough formula, there are two ways of measuring ingredients: one is based on a total percentage of all ingredients, meaning that all ingredients are a percentage of the total; the other is baker's percent, where flour is set at 100 percent and all other ingredients are a percentage of the flour. To illustrate this, let's use a list of accepted ranges for dough formulation:

ITEM	BAKER'S %
Flour	100%
Water	55-65%
Salt	1-2%
Sugar	1-5%
Yeast	.5-3%
Oil	1-14%

Other additives include milk, eggs, variations of oil such as olive oil, and a whole array of herbs, including popular garlic. In fact, you can pretty much add whatever you want to enhance the flavor profile of your crust, and you can either add your basil or oregano during mixing or just before topping the crust via sprinkling or spreading on with a brush.

Beware of using flavored powders, though, particularly when mixing the dough. There's more power in the powder than it appears, and too much of a good thing can detract from an otherwise great pizza.

Other chemical enhancements are also available, such as gums, and can be used to greatly alter a dough's characteristics. Ever wonder how a Tony's frozen pizza can crisp up so quickly in a home oven, and stay crispy for quite a while afterward, while your scratch-made pie—baked in a commercial workhorse of an oven—won't stay crisp for five minutes? Think additives and enhancements.

There are some natural dough conditioners that can be added to a dough to achieve specific results. Using a blend of whey and L-cysteine, mixing time is decreased and workability is increased. Another example is vital wheat gluten, which is a powder added right to the flour to increase the protein level of the flour. For further details on the many offerings in this vein, consult the wonderful resources in the back of the book.

Making dough from a pre-mix bag is the same as scratch, with one exception: all the ingredients, minus the water, is already thrown together in a bag. Basically, you're opening the bag into a mixing bowl and adding water. Many companies will mix these bags on a proprietary basis at your call, naturally after a few visits to their test kitchens to perfect it. This is a very handy alternative to doing it the "old fashioned way" and still maintaining control over your dough formulation.

Frozen dough has been around for a long time, but only within the last decade has it become widespread in American pizzerias. The reason for this is because of advanced production methods and formulations. For example, even five years ago you were hard-pressed to find a quality frozen pizza in grocery stores; today the grocers' freezers are packed with all sorts of varieties and brands. In fact, the frozen pizza segment breached $2.5 billion in sales, and constituted the fastest-growing segment in 2000.

Is it because of better ingredients? Maybe so, in a small way. The major advantage has been in the dough. Thin, traditional and deep-dish are available, and the self-rising dough is the star. DiGiorno from Kraft is the leader of the grocery frozen pizza group, a real growth engine: since its 1995 debut, the DiGiorno line increased from $545 million to nearly $1 billion in sales. As of the first printing of this book, the line posted a 6.8 percent net growth over its 2000 fiscal year. Kraft also runs the Tombstone and Jack's brands, and became cohorts in California Pizza Kitchen's efforts to push its gourmet pizza line in the frozen world. That has, of course, also been highly successful.

Schwan's and its Freschetta self-rising pizza (which incidently launched shortly after DiGiorno in '95) is the second largest market-holder, and grew 8.5 percent in its last full fiscal year.

Since this is the only place in this book we'll be discussing commercially frozen pizza, I can't fail to mention some of the other improvements that have contributed to this segment's recent burst of business. Because the processing clients have continuously requested more varieties of frozen pizza (unbaked crusts, unbaked fully-topped crusts, parbaked, etc.), equipment has been developed over the years to accommodate the demand.

One of the big recent improvements in frozen pizza production is continuous band technology, which maintains the structure of the dough as it's processed. This allows for a low-stress band of dough, which results in a softer and better quality finished product. This is what led to the development of the self-rising crust.

Other production improvements include new

relaxed-dough processor and sheeter designs, which allow for greater absorption and higher fermentation doughs to be fermented without using oil. For the processors, this means less mess, less down time. For the end product, this means a tastier dough and a lighter crust—closely resembling restaurant dough.

Some big pizza restaurant players haven't left the increased quality of frozen dough fall to the wayside; Domino's uses frozen for all its shell needs (and has for some time), as does Pizza Hut, who widely uses frozen pucks for its personal pans as well as their hand-tossed crust. The benefits of going frozen is seen immediately in labor savings, and food costs can be very similar. When you compare the production steps of making dough from scratch and using frozen pre-portioned patties or shells, it seems a no-brainer on paper. Where prep cooks had been arriving to work at 6 a.m. to begin mixing dough, and then begin the cycle of cutting, weighing, rounding and shaping over and over until all the dough was ready for the day, frozen dough creates a one-person job done even quicker.

In addition, there is no dough bowl and mixer to clean and maintain. In fact, for those companies fervently franchising, negating a dough mixer purchase—and possibly a rounder, divider or sheeter, all expensive equipment— is an attractive option. Also, in terms of shelf-life, frozen is an excellent option. Frozen dough has a shelf life of 12-18 weeks.

But what really sells folks on the pucks (or pallets, or shells) is the fact that a frozen portion is the same, one after another. In reality, there may be slight differences, but nothing compared to what is commonly seen with scratch batches. The commercial suppliers and commissaries that produce the dough, and then shape and flash-freeze the portions, are dealing with huge batches almost continuously. I've seen these operations pump out dough, and it's absolutely incredible. The shaping equipment (rounders, sheeters and rollers) monitor the size and shape and weight of the dough as it's conveyed through the line, making the error margin very slim.

Parbaked pizza crust is just what the name implies: the dough is partially cooked, and is the "ready to use" type of our lists of crusts. The masses are familiar with this type of product, associating it with Boboli in many grocery store delis. The ready-to-use idea is the main reason for its popularity with some operations, as practically all the prep steps are eliminated.

Although convenience is king, there is a significant downside to using a parbaked crust, that being it's twice-baked—first at the commissary where it's baked and packaged, second in your kitchen for finishing off as the end product. Twice-baking eliminates a lot of water content in the dough, resulting in a dry and often less tasty end product. One way to improve the flavor is to brush the crust lightly with flavored oil just before topping it.

Parbaked crusts are handy for those crusts that typically have longer proof times, such as thick or deep-dish pie crusts, which range from 25 to 75 minutes. These crusts are easily stacked either in walk-in cooler space or even on racks at room temperature, and inconsistencies are avoided because there is minimal handling. These factors are a Godsend when the rush of customers hit you on a Friday night and 90 percent of them want deep dish. No need for taking one or two people off the makeline to dash back and make more dough—instead, they're pulling off a rack and topping.

Parbaked crusts are also used at non-traditional sites, such as in kiosks in stadiums, where there's no room for extra freezer space for frozen crusts, and certainly no room for a mixer and dry storage. This means less equipment costs when opening up a smaller unit. Labor is also cut way back, as a small shop can easily turn into a one-man show, with no need for a full-time dough prepper.

I witnessed a lot of changes in my decade in operations pertaining to dough prep. I began mixing dough by scratch, weighing all the ingredients, stirring the yeast in warm water in the mixing bowl before adding the rest. Then came the pre-mix bags, first in 10-pound bags, and then in more convenient five-pound bags. Just add water and you were good to go. Eventually, we had arrived at an almost completely dummy-proof stage in high-volume dough prep. There were the pre-mix bags, complemented by an automatically heated water source (heated to exactly 105 degrees every time!), as well as frozen dough disks for certain sizes of pan pizzas.

Not only was labor saved with all this streamlining, but food costs improved dramatically. This is until a sleepy prep cook forgot if he'd put two or three pitchers of water in the bowl, and whether the dough had been set to mix for 10 minutes or 15. Inconsistencies are still out there, even with the technologies. Getting back to the basics is important, not because everyone will eventually be prepping dough from scratch again, but because preppers will be empowered to recognize why dough behaves a certain way. And early morning troubleshooting won't require throwing entire batches of dough out or calling the boss before the sun's up.

Foundations of Forming: It's a Toss-up

I remember a little Noble Romans shop that was just down the street from one of the Pizza Huts under my care. Call me a dastardly competitor for saying so, but I considered their pizza inferior to mine and there wasn't a comparison on the service level. But I began to experience some warning signals—more cars in front of their place than in my parking lot. Upon closer examination I noticed a large percentage—like, almost all—of the people coming and going had kids in tow.

One early evening I paid a visit to the Noble Romans incognito, and found out what the draw was. Kids were lined up to watch the pizza man behind a large enclosed pane of plexiglass tossing dough. They pointed, giggled, some of them mesmerized, some of them excited. It was live entertainment, and I would've laid down money that said they went home that night and begged mom to make some dough so they could toss it.

The hand-tossing pizza guy is an icon of the pizza world—at least in the public's eyes. There's certainly an amount of show involved, but there's also a useful element in the action. When you toss (or, as some call it, spin) dough, a flexible dry skin is formed as it twirls through the air with the greatest of ease, stretching to whatever diameter you desire. Tossing also rounds out the diameter of the crust, with the ideal rounded or "soft" edges that make for a perfect frame for your pie.

Mechanical shaping, as with dough rollers, sheeters, presses, and to an extent rounders, all work to produce a consistent shape to your dough. For speed and consistency, mechanical shaping is a widely accepted choice. Dough rollers and sheeters, purchased new, will run you $1,000 to $3,000 each; dough presses (either hot presses—which also produce parbaked crusts—and cold) will cost from $1,500 to $5,000. Dough-shaping equipment requires frequent cleaning and preventative maintenance, although fairly minimal.

Whatever method you choose to use to shape your crust, it's important to know how to avoid dough tearing or ripping. The more dough is handled, the more there's a chance of ruining it. Protein content of flour, as we've talked about before, is responsible for your dough's durability and elasticity. Similar to a rubber band, you want your dough to be able to stretch without breaking, but not so much that it pulls back (this is called "snap back"). Trying to work a dough to the edge of a pan during dough prep can be a frustrating nightmare when there's too much snap back.

With hand-pressed, slapped or tossed dough, there's very little disruption of the cell structure in the dough. To get an idea of what cell structure is, break a saltine cracker in half and look at the cross section of the break. See the tiny bubbles, or pockets? Those are cells, and the cell structure is what stabilizes, or creates, the dough form. Dough not introduced to much mechanization (i.e., running through a sheeter) bakes out with more height, all things equal. The dough is also more tender-eating.

With pressed dough, you get many smaller cells in the center of the dough. This is due to the gas cells being rearranged during the forming operation. There's a little toughening of the dough during the forming process, but not much. When sheeting the dough, you essentially de-gas the dough which results in a lower volume, or height, crust, unless it's proofed before baking. Because of the amount of work put into the dough during the sheeting process, the dough tends to be tougher.

Getting to the root of the matter—the ingredients—where's the happy median?

Use a high-protein content (13 to 14 percent is good), and include some sort of lubricant, like oil or shortening, to the level of 2 to 5 percent in your formulation. More than 5 percent will tend to weaken the gluten, and weak gluten in your dough means it'll tear too easily. Also, as we'd talked about earlier, using the right amount of salt will make for a strong dough. Never go above the 2-percent mark, as your gluten will then become too tough, and then you're into the snap-back scenario. Go about 1.5 to 1.7 percent salt in your formula and you won't go wrong.

You'll find that the longer a dough is fermented, already portioned and balled and under controlled conditions such as in a walk-in cooler, the easier it will be to shape. Of course, there's a limit to the amount of time as well, but as a general guide, don't expect your from-scratch dough to perform well beyond a three-day window. You'll also find that flavor from alcohol-producing yeast has more time to enrich the dough.

There is a risk using the rollers and sheeters, as I've personally witnessed people accidentally putting their hands too deep into the hopper. It wasn't a pretty sight. To the machines' credit, though, safety bars prevent most potential injuries, and they have improved over the years in that respect.

For that matter, I've also seen a guy reach for a batch of dough in a 60-quart mixer before the hook had completed its cycle, jerking in his hand, then his arm … I'll save you any further details, but I'll tell you he's lucky to be able to write with that hand today. My point is, dough-prep equipment is all safe, it's how that equipment is respected and used that usually results in injury. After all, we have laws that protect our kids from injuring themselves because by and large they're irresponsible and don't understand how dangerous some equipment or tasks can be.

In short, if you're making dough from scratch, you can't live without dough production equipment. Every piece becomes your partner in the business, and most pieces, if taken care of with preventative maintenance, will be workhorses. They'll last a long, long time. But make sure the kids working around them are responsible, and if they can use the machinery, let them know how valuable it is to your business.

What You'll Need Equipment-wise

If you'll be making dough from scratch, you have a few choices in terms of mixing equipment. A dough mixer runs second only to your ovens in terms of top-dollar investment, so spend wisely. First off, know that there are dough mixers, and there are pizza dough mixers. The difference is that for a pizza dough mixer, you'll need plenty of horsepower due to the toughness of the dough. You're not mixing muffin batter—or at least I hope you're not! In fact, the stiffer and tougher your dough is, the more horsepower you'll need to mix it.

With planetary mixers (the primarily larger ones, with three or four legs supporting a top dome-shaped motor and a hanging bowl), a good rule to go by when determining how much power you'll need is: for every 13-

15 pounds of dough mixing, you need one horsepower. You'll find plenty of use in a three- or four-horsepower mixer, which usually has a 60-quart capacity.

There are two types of machinery in planetary mixers: gear-driven and belt-driven motors. While gears are durable, when they do putt out they're expensive to replace, whereas a belt is relatively easy and cheap to replace. The only bad thing (and it's a doozy) is that when a belt snaps, the mixing motor continues to run and can ruin the finer workings.

With gear-driven mixers, keep them oiled with an 80- to 90-weight gear oil, and they'll last you a long time. Another type of mixer is the vertical-cutter mixer (VCM), which cuts the dough with vertical blades. The advantage to VCMs is the speed they can mix dough. A batch of dough that would take a planetary mixer 6 minutes to mix can be mixed by a VCM in almost a quarter the time.

While the planetary mixer is found in the majority of American pizzerias, both varieties are durable and come highly recommended. My advice: talk with everyone in the field, and ask to see demos either at existing stores or at their facilities.

Another large piece of equipment needed for fresh dough production is a proofer (otherwise known as a proofing cabinet, or hot box). There's a wide range of proofers on the market; my experience has been with insulated models, which, in my opinion, is the only way to go. Proofers are heated cabinets in which dough is housed to proof (allowing the yeast time to cause the dough to rise in a controlled environment), the temperature which varies, but shouldn't go above 125 F.

Models range from $2,200 to $3,900, mainly

depending on if the proofer will double as a heating holding unit (with higher temperature and space capacity), double- or single-door, and whether it's insulated.

Although all dough doesn't need a controlled environment in which to proof (thin crust is one example) and may be fine to proof at room temperature, if you're dealing with frozen dough or any thick crusts, proofers are necessary.

Pizza Platitude #4

*One important key to success
is self-confidence. An important key
to self-confidence is preparation.*
Arthur Ashe (1943 - 1993) US tennis player,
AIDS spokesperson

5

Getting Sauced

As was discussed in the previous section, the sauce and dough share a precarious coexistence. If the relationship isn't balanced (that is, one or both are of poor quality or improperly prepared), the entire pizza's quality will suffer.

The Gum Line Isn't Chewy

One element of a pizza sauce that determines a sauce's consistency (its thinness and thickness) is its solids. Quality pizza sauces contain 16 to 20 percent solids—these are thick enough to hold a fork or spoon upright.

Sauces that contain less solid percents are thinner, and even soupy. And what happens when you apply it to dough? It separates. The tomato solids float to the top of the mixture, and the remaining water gravitates down into the dough. During baking, the crust heats up and a gummy, sticky layer forms right underneath the sauce. This is the gum line.

Gum lines form most often with deep-dish doughs, because many deep-dish recipes call for more sauce than thin or traditional pies. So when thinner sauce is applied to thicker dough, the sauce separates and results in more water on the crust. In addition, deep-dish dough is a softer, more impressionable dough, with a more open cell structure. If a shell is sauced too long before baking, the likelihood of sauce separation and consequent gum line increases. Thus the importance of waiting as soon as you'll be cooking the pie as possible.

The gum line is a result of an unbalanced relationship between dough and crust, where the moisture-retention barrier is a fine one, a fine line that's actually been an issue from pizza's get-go. Pizzeria operators have tried using vegetable parchment films to reduce the risk of water seeping into their crusts, but to no avail.

One thing that can help with gum-line problems, however, is oil application. Spreading or spraying a thin layer of vegetable oil over the surface of the dough works effectively as a moisture barrier, and it can also give the outside crust a golden appearance during cooking. But it won't guarantee a gumless dough.

The closest thing to a guarantee is using the appropriate amount of high-quality sauce with dough that can stand up to it. A little experimentation and trial and error helps, too.

Experienced pizza makers know that if you're topping a pie with moist toppings—ones that will "water out" during baking—such as peppers and tomatoes, a bit less sauce is in order.

If you like using sauce with chunks of tomatoes in the mix, beware of excessive watering out during the cooking process. It's wise to test each and every new sauce recipe on various dough types before using it full time.

As detrimental as a gum line is due to sub-standard dough prep or dough handling procedures, the same goes for a sauce that destroys a crust.

I've been the unfortunate manager on the other side of the counter of an irate customer, jabbing his finger at a sorry-looking, soggy pizza in a red-tinted box. After leaving with his carryout pizza (a large pan, loaded, I'll never forget), he backed out of his parking space, only to watch the pizza slosh from the passenger seat to the dash, and then to the floor. With that explanation of events, you may turn around right now saying "Well, pity on you, Tracy—wow, that guy had it coming. Pulling out like a mad man. He deserved a mess..."

Well, there's more to the story! I'd seen badly banged-up pizza before, and it never looked like this. Sauce literally dripped from the box lid as he held it open—it looked like there had been 12 orders of over-sauced pasta thrown in there. Where were the toppings for crying out loud? I couldn't even determine what was on the pizza, except for SAUCE. A lot of it!

After surviving the fit of rage and taking care of the customer, my ears still ringing, I went back to investigate our sauce source. Sure enough, there on the make line stood a cook stirring pizza sauce in the sauce pan—the classic sign that something was wrong with it.

Concentrate had settled in the five-gallon buckets in the walk-in, and it was mixed that morning. The culprit—a lazy prep cook who didn't mind stirring sufficiently. Not only were the night-shift cooks compensating for sauce that was either too thin or too thick, depending on what stage they poured from the bucket, pockets of spices had gathered in select areas in the tomato concentrate. It was a lovely night.

Now, as an operator, you may come back and tell me it was just as much the fault of the cooks on the make line for not stirring the sauce while still in the bucket ... wherever the fault lie, one thing's for sure—a bad sauce job is a bad sauce job when the customer gets a pizza with a bad sauce job. Put the finest, freshest ingredients on top-shelf crust, but screw up the sauce and the whole thing's a waste!

Who's On First (Base)?

Pizza sauce is considered the "base" sauce of the pie. Think of it this way: the dough is the foundation, and the sauce is the base on which the toppings are placed. The base gives the pizza maker a frame in which she can create her work of art, a guide of sorts. In fact, when topping a pizza with ingredients, you can use the base's outside edge to draw a distinct line where the toppings and cheese stop. This, of course, is for pizza that has an outside crust (or, a clean crust). This outside crust is also called the lip, or the handle.

The trick to a great pizza sauce is matching its attributes to the crust and your intended taste. Keep in mind that a thicker sauce will make it more difficult to spread over the surface of the dough. This makes for potential devastation during a busy period, especially for thicker doughs, like deep-dish pan pizza dough. It's a good idea to allow this type of dough to cool for a substantial amount of time after proofing, since applying sauce on a dough with a skin (witnessed as yeast slows its activity, an effect of cooling) is much more efficient and less risky.

Consistencies and World Peace

So should all pizza sauces possess a soupy consistency? Not at all—there are as many sauce consistencies as there are dough types. The secret is experimenting with different combinations of dough and sauce. At one time during my years in operations, we used three different sauces, all with their own spices and consistencies, with four different dough types. I recommend, however, settling on one or two pizza sauces. This sticks in my memory because of the mess and hassle of handling too many sauces—and the inconsistencies found on the makeline when I wasn't around.

You'll find that if a dough doesn't have a raised lip (or a ridge) around the outside edge, and you apply too thin of a sauce, the pie will push out the sauce as it cooks, and you'll end up with burnt sauce dripping over the edges. This is especially detrimental to customers' palates and eye appeal if your pies are supposed to feature clean handles.

Another result of poorly planned sauce is a pizza sauce that's too thick. The result is often under-cooked dough, and the aforementioned gum line. Avoid having to troubleshoot and fix cookability problems early on in your product development—get your sauce right!

Scratch or Packaged?

As with most things in life, you have a choice with your pizza sauce. Some operators are diehard sauce-from-scratch fanatics, and with good reason—you're able to add to or take away from any sauce you conjure up. If you decide to thicken a sauce, you know what you need to do; same goes for thinning it, or adjusting spice amounts.

Some argue that red sauce made from scratch has better flavor due to less work done outside their own kitchens, including the heating factor. Tomatoes that are heated too much, as in some processing where they're cooked up to four separate times, results in a degraded, less tomatoey flavor. Fresh-packed tomatoes are usually only cooked once, and are canned soon after harvest. Obviously this is something to consider with your red sauces. The only downside to fresh-packed is the cost, which typically runs about 5 to 10 percent higher than remanufactured sauces.

Many operators begin with tomato concentrate, mixing spices, oil and water to spec for their pizza sauce. Some will also heat the sauce before using to ensure an even flavor distribution, usually when oil is added. Pizza sauce can be enhanced with fresh basil leaf, olive oils, and other items such as sugar. Sugar actually has a common use in pizza sauce, acting to tone down tomatoes' highly acidic nature. But beware of adding too much sugar, as the natural flavor of a tomatoey sauce can be skewed.

Cheeses like ricotta and mascarpone are added to some sauces to give a rich, creamy consistency and quite a zip to a pie. Vegetables, such as onions, peppers, carrots and celery, chopped fine, are also a popular enhancement, as are small amounts of other sauces, like Cajun or beef or chicken broths and stocks. Of course, these ingredients are used sparingly, since they're only intended to enhance, not overtake, the flavor and texture of the pizza sauce.

The case for pre-prepped (or ready-to-use) sauce includes thoughts of consistency, convenience and labor savings. The 16-year-old kid can open the can or pouch, pour it in the pan, and the next pie's ready to be made. There's also the reduced inventory; instead of all the ingredients needed for a scratch recipe, it's all in one container.

The cost for pre-prepped sauces can be as much as 20 cents more for a 16-inch pizza, depending on if your sauce is a proprietary brand or not.

During a tour of a nearby sauce manufacturer, I found out that the newest trend is a unique approach to sauce prep called "speed scratch". Speed scratch sauces are those sauces that are packed, ready to use with all the ingredients minus a few items, which are vacuum-sealed in packets and opened during in-store prep. The result is a unique flavor from a pre-prepped sauce.

Here, using speed scratch, even the most die-hard homegrown cooks can live with something that comes out of a factory. He (or she) can whip up something that can be called their own, even if some of the ingredients were heated some during the process.

Packaging Know-how: Pouches, Cans and Tree-huggers

There was a day when all tomato products came packed in #10 metal cans. Cans are still widely used, but the advent of plastic pouches has brought another option to the operator. With pouches, you're able to remove them from the case and store in walled racks, thereby reducing storage space, as opposed to using up rack space with cans.

There's also the risk of cuts with opening, scraping and cleaning cans, as there will invariably be a sharp edge that will be the cause of a band-aid or two.

Pouches also reduce waste. Instead of filling a dumpster with empty cans, pouches can be crumpled and stuffed into a trash can. Again, because of the convenience, the cost is slightly higher with pouches versus cans. An intangible cost, however, can always be recouped, by casting a favorable light on your environmental consciousness—reducing waste and thinking of your local landfill capacity. Okay, maybe you're not thinking of landfills, but at least it feels and looks good. A more direct benefit may be reduced visits from the trash collectors.

Even with cans you can be environmentally smart. If you're using cans, ask your trash collection company if they supply containers for recyclable materials—most do these days. Fill those smaller dumpsters up, and although you may still pay for extra pickups, at least you're coming out smelling like a rose.

Sauces Are Not All of One Race, Creed or Color

In this chapter we've been talking of red sauce—the traditional pizza sauce. With the diverse palate of the world's taste buds (actually an enriched taste now shared among more groups of people as travel is more extensive and cultures are readily shared), varieties of sauce are now in vogue.

Take the white pizza, prepared with a "white sauce". What the white sauce consists of depends on who's cooking. An actual white sauce is made up of fat or butter, flour, milk, cream, or stock, and seasoning. Here's a white lie I'll share with you: Some "white" pizzas I've seen are anything made with a sauce that happens to be white (i.e., alfredo sauce, mayonaise). And why not? So far the pizza police haven't taken these operators away, and I suggest that if it feels good, do it! Having either a true white sauce or another sauce that's white, and calling it your own white pizza, makes the pizza stand out on your menu, and any way it's made it's sure to be unique.

(On a personal note, one of my favorite all-around pies is a thin-crust mayo-based creation with chicken, red onion, a smattering of mozzarella, topped with real bacon pieces and a few jalepenos. If you make me one of these when I visit your town next, you'll have a friend for life, and I'll chase away any white pizza purists from your shop!)

Barbecue sauce has made some inroads as well, usually acting as the base for chicken pies—the flavor profile of these two match well, and it has an easy name: BBQ Chicken. Americans can relate. Again, there are some who prefer to make this sauce from scratch, as with red sauce. But to be able to avoid the sticky, sugary mess, I suggest purchasing the sauce in easy-to-pour ready-to-use bottles. Barbecue sauce isn't usually cheap, but the good thing is the stuff lasts forever when refrigerated, and you need only use a small amount on a pizza—too much and you've got more barbecue than pizza per bite.

Other sauce varieties include pesto, refried beans for pizzas like Mexican or "taco" pizzas, or even squid ink (believe it) that's popular in Japan.

And then there are some pies made without any sauce at all. Some chefs simply brush a little butter or crushed garlic on as an ultra-thin base and top with ingredients. This acts more to create a slight barrier between topping and crust than anything—well, taste has a lot to do with it, too!

With all the sauces used as pizza base, you should be able to apply it with at least one other menu item. Red sauce is easily used cross-platform with pasta dishes; white sauce the same (the real white sauce as well as alfredo); barbecue can be used with wings, or a dip for appetizers, such as chicken fingers.

I've learned that whatever your sauce profile, and from whatever slant you lean—'homemade or the highway', or 'canned works fine'—there's some culinary talent in the best packing plants. By culinary talent, I mean folks that work in the plants that have jobs because they know how to help pizza men and women like us.

Many of these people have culinary backgrounds (chefs, caterers, culinary arts school graduates, etc.) and hold titles similar to consultant or account liaison. Need a special blend? No problem with the packing plants with good reputations; they just sick their food guy on the project, and there are great extents of time and talent to make you happy.

Pizza Platitude #5

To get profit without risk, experience without danger, and reward without work, is as impossible as it is to live without being born. A. P. Gouthey

---

6

Pizza Guys and the Zen of Cooking

Because the root of the business is about making pizza, it's no surprise that how the pizza is made is at the top of most operator's priorities and pride. Thus far we've talked about the magic found in dough, the importance that sauce plays, and the various combinations that create the matrix found on menus. This chapter focuses on how the product is cooked--or, more accurately, baked.

The reason pizzas made at home (even those made from scratch dough and the freshest ingredients) aren't comparable to shop-made pies can be blamed on the type of oven used. Although there have been some recent technological breakthroughs in baking processes with home ovens and ranges, the baking procedure of commercial pizza ovens is unmatched. These ovens were created and are manufactured with one thing in mind--how to cook pizza. And there's a lot that goes into it, certainly more than just being able to melt the mozz and crisp the crust.

There are issues of "cookability" of a pie, the ability for appropriate cooking temperatures to fully penetrate topping, sauce and dough. Cooking speed is also critical in these days of the no-wait philosphy of customer service and the public's desire for near-instant gratification. An even bake is another factor of commercial ovens and a consistent quality.

Religious Convictions & Ovens

Because of the different types of ovens and the various methods these ovens use to cook the pie, operators draw tall walls around their personal preferences. Operators are so convinced that their oven is the only way to cook a pie that they'd rather face death than denounce it. I venture to say that no other single issue—of what type of oven to use—holds such conviction as this.

So, if you seek advice on which type of oven to use, expect some thoughts of absolution and a "my way or the highway" attitude. Remember, you're talking about finishing off your prized possession, and no other oven or method will do! And, of course, the oven manufacturers won't argue with their clients' convictions.

The different types of ovens include deck, wood-burning, coal-burning, gas/wood-burning combination, conveyors, and hybrid models. All these types of ovens use similar baking physics to get the job done, based on what the oven is engineered to do.

Deck ovens utilize heated stone (thus, a stone 'deck') to cook pizza, taking heat from the stone to cook slowly and, what deck users will tell you on their death bed, results in a superior crust. And there may be some truth in this conviction: the ingredients in the dough are allowed to bake from the outer surface up, and with a little more time develops a flavor unlike a crust baked in other types of ovens.

The traditional make-up of the deck and lining in

deck ovens were asbestos stones, but after laws passed a few years ago prohibiting the use of asbestos in ovens, many other compounds have been used. Many tenured pizza makers believe these new stones are less reliable as asbestos, especially in maintaining heat. But those that use decks with conviction will tell you that it's the evenly distributed heat of a deck oven that allows their pie to cook so well. Even if a steel hearth is used (usually with pies in pans or on screens) where the heat transfer is faster, the taste difference remains.

To be sure, before there were any other types of ovens, there were decks. But today's "deck oven" is either heated with gas or electrically, cooking at a constant 600 F to 700 F. Much has changed since the early 1900s, when New York pizza makers raked hot coal fires across the baking deck of huge brick ovens. Or has it? Operationally, maybe, but with decks, the pizza cooks the same—just a little quicker.

Basically, with a deck oven, you're cooking in a baking chamber with a hearth. The hearth is heated from beneath, which, for gas models, contains burners. For electric models, heat comes from a bottom set of heating elements attached to the bottom side of the deck and a second set at the top of the cooking chamber. Then there's the ventilation stack for gas models—electric models have no combustible gases, therefore no need for ventilation. Pretty simple.

The benefit, other than a great bake, is that decks are the workhorses of the industry, with a truly dependable reputation. Also, there's no wood to burn and a fire to maintain, as well no zoning issues to fight, which we'll talk about shortly.

Despite their dependability, there are some down-sides to using decks. For one, opening and closing the door cools down the first few inches of the cooking deck. The further back in the oven, the hotter it gets. It's important for deck oven-tenders to understand the heating properties of the oven and work the pies around the deck, finding hot spots for quicker cook times.

The escaping heat also contributes to a hot kitchen quickly, and in smaller shops heat up the dining room as well. Adequate training time for a deck-oven tender can be substantial, and the margin for error can be a wide one. Keep in mind the people you wish to concentrate your training efforts when considering purchasing a deck oven. Wood-burning ovens, which also bake pizza on a stone deck, are usually lined with refractory stone, which commonly arches in the interior.

The stone hearth has a very warm and inviting aesthetic appeal, and combined with the soft glow of burning wood inside creates an ambiance all its own. I've been to many stores that have featured wood-burning ovens as the centerpiece of their operations, positioned where customers are drawn to it and can see from all angles.

From a practical standpoint, traditional wood-burning ovens pack a lot of thermal mass in its upper arch and can maintain high temperatures thanks to its thick stone lining, which can be as thick as six inches. Internal temperatures can reach up to 850 F, with the stack of wood (the stacking method is a science in and of itself) burning at designated stages and positions, atop the surface of the hearth. I've seen wood stacked on one side, in the far rear, or on both sides. It seems that wherever it's stacked, the dry heat from the burning wood cooks pies much faster than a gas-fueled oven.

Pizza baked in a wood-burning oven has a tinge of the taste of wood which cooks it, offering a rustic flavor. Pizza makers use specific types of wood for specific fragrance, lighting capability and burning longevity, along with other factors. Of course, since wood is the only fuel source, it's important to find a reliable distribution channel. No wood, no fire. No fire, no pizza. No pizza ... well, you get my point. Plan to monthly burn one to two cords of hardwood for a moderate- to large-sized oven.

How is using a wood-burning oven perceived within the industry? In the United States, we can look at chains like California Pizza Kitchen and Bertucci's and judge for ourselves how the public and other operators view the success of the presence and use of these ovens. Some are even predicting that the next big trend in frozen, commercial pizza will be pizza (or at least the crust) that's par-baked in a wood-burning oven, then frozen.

Look in Italy and you'll see that religious zeal I mentioned ... to the point of defying authority, actually. Roughly seven million pizzas are consumed each day in that country, most finished off in wood-burning ovens. The European Union began handing down some fairly strict food safety guidelines to be implemented in Italy's traditional shops, calling for switching to electric or gas ovens. The reason: so food wouldn't come into contact with the ashes from the burning wood. The reaction: "Don't touch our ovens!" Italian lawmakers are now in the process of introducing legislation that permanently protects the time-honored way of pizza baking. I'd say that's a vote of earned respect for the wood-burning models.

Coal-burning ovens are those well-respected and

rare artifacts of pizza's roots. Found only in the older cities on the East coast (New York, Boston), one day they'll be gone. But not forgotten. Pollution has a lot to do with increasingly strict zoning measures, and why there are only a few coal-burning ovens left in the United States. In these cities, you're unable to open a restaurant and use such an oven due to the excessive CO_2 and the gas's detriment to the environment. But, oh, the pizza that comes from one!

The rich flavor that infiltrates the crust, cheese and toppings is unlike any other. Native New Yorkers know where the coal ovens are, and there's rarely a slow night at these legendary locations. Hot coals are shoveled onto the cooking deck of the oven, and the pie is cooked with the same heating dynamics as the wood-burning models. These brick ovens cook pizza quickly, with some of the highest temperatures in commercial pizza ovens.

To my knowledge, because of the stringent environmental laws, especially in the larger cities, and the public outcry for the resultant pollution these ovens create, there aren't any coal-burning ovens in production in the states. When a restaurant with a coal-burning oven in residence—not necessarily a pizzeria—goes up for sale, people who know pizza and what the oven can do for it flock to the place and place bids. It's an incredible thing to see, and yet sad that the aroma and taste hasn't been replicated by another cooking method.

Gas/wood-burning combination ovens give an operator the best of both worlds. You've got the look and feel (ambiance creators) of the traditional wood-burning oven, without some of the hassles, such as those evil combustible gases. There's no more waiting for two hours for a fire; by flipping a switch you have even heat at the ideal temperature without having to keep an eye on the fire—maintaining the embers and stoking it as time allows. As far as the wood goes, forget about scouting for a reliable source of fair-priced hardwood, and there's no worry in terms of additional storage space for next cord or two or disposing of the hot ashes at night.

Some operators have gone with gas combination ovens to offset the cost of fuel—in this case, the expensive fuel being choice cuts of wood. In these energy-starved days, however, with the recent crisis at hand, gas is the more expensive option. That goes doubly for pizzerias. Gas/wood-burning combo units can take anywhere from 50,000 BTUs for a smaller oven to close to 180,000 BTUs for large model.

As far as comparing these units to a traditional wood-burning unit, there are also burners and thermostat controls which need serviced. Traditional wood-burning ovens, on the other hand, have no mechanical parts.

Conveyor ovens cook with convection heat, which is blown via fan-forced air. The effect this intense, blowing heat has on a pizza is to remove the colder-air layer which envelopes the pie. As the conveyor belt, made of steel links, pulls the pie through the oven, the pie passes through cooking zones which all have different temperatures, and sometimes different angles of blowing air. Some conveyor ovens avoid convection altogether, using instead a mix of gas and electric heat. These types are usually a slower cook, but result in more moist pizzas.

Many inside the industry, both on the oven manufacturing side and the operator side, say that the technology in conveyors has improved so much the past few years that you're not able to tell the difference between a conveyor-cooked pizza and a deck-baked one. Of course, the deck people will argue, and things get a little sticky. (No, you're not reading the dough chapter.)

Of all the ovens, conveyors are the "dummy-proof" of the industry, which speaks volumes to operators struggling with high-schoolers with the wrong idea of an open-door policy. With conveyors, once the pizza is made, it goes on the belt and comes out a finished product. Training time is a fraction of that for deck ovens—there's no "babying" the pizza. Of course, like with any oven, there's the visual checks for bubbles as the pie cooks, but by and large it's an over-simplified process.

Conveyors also afford the operator a consistent bake every time, and for those growing companies out there, this also speaks volumes. Other benefits include cooler kitchens, reduced burn incidents, and increased labor efficiency, as kitchen employees can jump to another job after a pizza is placed on the belt. This, compared to an oven-tender at a deck oven, who is usually glued to the oven through a pie's baking cycle.

Hybrids are ovens that feature a combination of certain types of ovens mentioned above. For instance, there's a combination deck oven with conveyor, or an "air deck oven", which has been on the market for about 12 years. This oven replaces the stone floors with screens and uses forced air to cook the pizza, otherwise known as convection heat. Okay, that word 'convection' popped up again, and it's a physics term ... I suppose this is an appropriate segue to—

Advanced Cooking Technologies

Remember sitting in your high school physics class,

drifting off as you thought, "There's not a snowball's chance I'm ever going to use this stuff."? Well, guess what—now you've got your chance!

For the past couple decades, Lincoln, one of the top conveyor companies, held the patent on a heating/baking technology called 'impingement'. In a nutshell, impingement resembles convection, where heated air (we're talking in the 450 to 650 F range) is forced through holes positioned throughout the oven's baking chamber. Whereas convection heat blows air across the pizza to speed the cooking process, impingement blows air through holes at various angles. The heated air is also constantly circulated and recycled throughout the chamber as the metal "fingers" (rectangular compartments through which air is forced) vacuumed, re-heated, and forced back through.

Lincoln uses this technology effectively in their conveyor ovens, smothering pizzas as they pass through the different cooking zones. The result is a fast and furious bake—thoroughly cooked to your liking as long as the temperature and belt speed are set accurately.

Last year the impingement patent was up for grabs, and just like with Alex Bell, others got into the game; instead of AT&T and Sprint, though, you have Lincoln and some other oven pros using impingement with other baking sources.

General Electric introduced some pretty impressive twists on light usage in cooking, and made it affordable enough to put in home ovens last year. Used largely in combo with convection cooking, light is "infused" on product and cooked in incredibly short time periods. We're talking a T-bone in three minutes--and it's well done! This really isn't a breakthrough, however, because infrared's been around for a while and used in cooking. The neat thing about GE's new light technology, though, is that if you placed your hand under the light rays, there's no sensation of heat. When you operate ovens that don't get hot, many benefits arise: a constantly cool kitchen, relieving cooks and patrons; low maintenance costs, as compressors or motors are less apt to overheat; utility bills are lower, particularly in the summer, when you battle with keeping the restaurant cool.

FlashBake is another product that uses "lightwave" technology, penetrating pizza with radiant heat. This technology is actually based on the same type of high-intensity light involved in manufacturing semiconductors.

TurboChef came out with an oven that used impingement technology combined with microwave to speed up the cooking process—that company boasts that it can cook about 45 16-inch pizzas an hour.

Amana has an oven that uses microwave energy and a powerful wallop of convection that can cook a frozen, par-baked pizza in just over three minutes.

Lincoln also has a combination impingement/ microwave oven that cranks out pizzas and other products quickly and thoroughly.

Pizza, hot sandwiches, subs, chicken wings — all hot menu items. But let's assume that these are the only four items that you want to serve. Maybe you're in a food court or simple deli operation where a limited menu is a requirement (space considerations might also come into play). Maybe you want to speed up your carryout service.

One thing is sure: You want the items done quickly.

The equipment consideration here is one of the new high-speed ovens (several styles are available from various manufacturers). A combination of convection and microwave energy, these ovens are the answer when fast cooking is required.

Fresh pizza bakes in three minutes, chicken wings in about the same amount of time. Even more interesting: The roll of, say, a sub sandwich can be toasted while the cheese inside is getting melted; all of this takes about 90 seconds. These ovens are ideal where space is a problem. The downside is that they can be expensive (range is $3,000 to $5,000, depending on model and manufacturer), but in the right situation the oven could pay for itself in no time.

Will these supped-up ovens ever take the place of the bigger boys? Never. But they can act as the perfect supplement in a busy kitchen that needs help with side orders and some relief from packed ovens. Most of these models mentioned above—and others not mentioned—have small footprints and fit practically anywhere. Plus, there's no exhaust, so no worries about additional ventilation. These pieces are also perfect for the non-traditional location (kiosk, arena concessions, etc.) that needs a very fast cook time with minimal installation.

Test Kitchens and Cookability Hot Spots

Many oven manufacturers host one or more test kitchens at their facilities. The reason this is a big plus for you, the operator in search either a new oven or additional ovens, is that you're allowed to bring in your own product and bake it off. Not only will you be able to tinker with the adjustments to "get it just right", but you'll learn a lot in the process. As your pie bakes, say, through a conveyor, you'll have the answers when pies begin coming out with stripes, or with only one half baked thoroughly. Believe me, it's not as easy as increasing or reducing the temperature.

I know of some oven manufacturers that are outstanding in their pursuit of end-user training. One company's test kitchen facilities include a bank of walls with at least a dozen brick ovens, where users are encouraged to test their product. Keep in mind that a lot more goes into actually cooking a pie in a wood-burning oven, compared to a conveyor, such as turning the pie during cooking, and moving from one hot spot to another.

Proving true to my non-biased disclaimer, I can't really say which oven type is better than the other--I've cooked and eaten pizzas from both, and every experience was efficient and tasty! But if you're serious about finding the perfect oven for you, test kitchens are the place to find out. Buying and installing your oven will be the most expensive equipment decision you'll make, and it'll pay to visit as many test kitchens as you can before buying.

It's also advisable to bring along a second set of eyes and hands to experience the test kitchen and the oven. This person should be one that will be minding the store when you're not around, someone that will be able to troubleshoot and maintain the oven as well as you.

Matching Your Crust With an Oven

When you think about how certain ovens cook, it's easier to make a decision on which oven to use by matching it to your type of pizza. Do you sell mainly thin crust pies? Or are you a Chicago native and believe only in stuffed pizza, or maybe you're a deep-dish person.

Generally speaking, thin crusts bake well on deck

ovens. This isn't to say thin pies aren't doable in other types, but the East Coast—primarily New York City—loves the charred appearance and unique taste that can only be acheived with a thin crust on a stone slab. The reason for this is primarily the extra sugar content in the dough that allows for the quick cook time on the hot stone. Logically, the thickness of the crust allows for fast cooking, as there's not as much substance to bake. Since thin crust is cracker-like, the cell structure is flat (snap a saltine in half and look at the cross section--the little air gaps or bubbles are cells) and smaller and therefore cooks quicker.

When a pizza cooks on a deck (whether it be gas, wood-fired, coal-fired, etc.), the stone on which it lies is hotter than the surrounding air. Thus the reason behind less amounts of topping on thinner crusts--go to Italy and you won't find gobs of cheese and sauce on their pizzas. Why? Mound the toppings on their thin crust and the bottom crust will be singed by the time the toppings are cooked. Yes, traditionally, they use deck ovens.

Conveyors are great for thicker crusts. Because the fingers, which distribute and blow out hot air, make up the cooking zones in an oven, are arranged above and below the pizza, the pie is simultaneously cooked from all directions. This allows for an even bake as the pie passes through, and can penetrate a thick crust and extra toppings efficiently.

Please note that these are generalizations. Some pizza pros have achieved great results from their ovens by fine-tuning them like a piano. And it's just as much an art form as music. I've witnessed some oven orchestrators posi- tion the embers in their wood-burning oven at the perfect spot, turning the pie at the perfect time, and serve a perfect thick-crust piled-high pie. God only knows how long it took for him to achieve that proficiency, though. Not that I don't believe I could eventually become as artistic, it's just that I'm not that patient of a guy.

Along this same line, the size of your menu may also be a determinant in an oven decision. Conveyors are built for speed and dummy-proofing the cooking process. Side dishes such as baked spaghetti or cavitini can easily be added to the product flow through the oven, and can usually be added further into the process via side window or door. An order of garlic cheese bread can be bumped ahead of a pizza by placing it on the conveyor for a two-minute bake, ahead of a pie placed at the rear of the belt with a seven-minute bake time.

Beware the jam-packed conveyor, however. Don't rely on your conveyor to cook everything, as the speed at which food rolls out can sometimes overwhelm even two or three people working the cut table. I grimace when I recall crazy Friday nights, pastas rolling out, side-swiping pizzas and breadsticks, only to perform double-gainers over the high-dive platform and crash land. Even worse were those lunches when personal pans were promoted with a frenzy at Pizza Hut, and what seemed like zillions of non-stop conveying action swamped me and my cut guys. The only way to avoid the crash and burn was to stack them, one atop another, as they came out.

For conveyor people, the solution's easy—add another conveyor. The ovens are easily stacked, sharing the same exhaust and power supply. I've seen as many as five conveyors stacked and used proficiently.

Deck users often find that their oven gets crowded quickly, and find side dishes troublesome. What I've seen used to avoid this traffic jam is the use of smaller ovens, such as microwaves and convections.

What You'll Pay

As I said before, purchasing and installing an oven will be your single most expensive equipment investment. So it pays to play the field and see what all is out there. Only you will know if a particular oven is the vehicle that cooks your pie the best.

Deck ovens, the least expensive of your oven choices, will run you in the neighborhood of $5,500-$7,500 for, say, a single 60-inch unit that's gas-powered. You can raise that price substantially with extras like more expensive or thicker tiles, copper exterior shell, and so on.

Wood-burning ovens are in the $5,500-$10,000 range, but may possibly run more if you're looking to spruce it up with colored exterior tile or other decorative accents.

Combo wood/gas units will cost you anywhere from $6,500-$18,000, depending on bells and whistles.

A typical conveyor will run you about $12,500-$15,000.

Leasing is an option that creates an affordable alternative for those without $15,000 lying around. Leasing also allows for a consistent maintenance schedule (depending on the company and the leasing agreement), and a way out if you find that maintenance and user friendliness isn't what you anticipated.

There's also the used and refurbished equipment route. I don't advise buying ovens (or other large pieces of equipment for that matter) at auctions. I've heard more bad than good from such buying endeavors, when twice and sometimes three times as much has been spent fixing and maintaining than what was spent at auction. There's rarely a warranty, and you never really know what you're getting. Companies that sell used and refurbished ovens, however, will stand behind their product. If you can live without a lengthier warranty and less shine, this is a very sensible route for you if finances don't allow for a new purchase.

Refurbished seems to be a new catch phrase with some of the "big boys" as well, such as Middleby Marshall, who's recently introduced its own line of refurbished ovens. Even the new oven guys realize the worth of yesterday's models, and not just for parts!

Pizza Platitude #6

Much of our American progress has been the product of the individual who had an idea; pursued it; fashioned it; tenaciously clung to it against all odds; and then produced it, sold it, and profited from it.

Hubert H. Humphrey

7

Powerful POS

Computerized point-of-sale (POS) systems is practically a necessity in today's pizza restaurant, no matter if the concept is delco or high-end full service. Technology must keep pace to capture orders as customer demand and complex menus rise in number. If you're wishing to cut a profit (and you do, otherwise you wouldn't be in the business or curious as to how to do so), you must have control over the flow of orders. This flow is coming in and going out of your shop, and it's critical to keep tabs on every segment.

This is especially true for those managing multiple units. In fact, the bigger you are or plan to be, the less control you have over this order flow. It follows that the bigger you are, the more necessary is a computerized POS system.

At its most basic, a POS system allows you to automate tasks which used to be handled manually. Such tasks include everything from counting a delivery driver's bank at the end of his shift and taking orders on order pads, to the whole gamut of administrative jobs: reports, cash till counts, payroll, inventory, etc. As with any other type of restaurant or retail environment, information is like gold, and it's up to you to get a handle on it, gathering it with powerful tools.

Managing a busy store also means the sooner the information is gathered, the sooner you can make informed decisions, such as: getting Sally off the cash register because of repeat shortages; order extra cheese on the next truck to avoid running out; don't schedule the extra prep cook to come in until 10:00 because labor is high or his time is unproductive; or staff the extra waitress to take care of the extra influx of patrons.

That's the type of power found at your fingertips when you utilize a POS system.

Controlling the Controllables With a Mouse Click

When you're talking about having a tight reign on your controllable costs, an automated POS system allows you to track the flow of business we talked about before. Here is where today's POS systems rise head and shoulders above what people used to consider computers in pizza shops—that is, expensive and glorified cash registers.

Computerized POS can have an enormously positive impact on cost savings in every major area of your business, including labor, inventory and cash control. Once used, every operator I've spoken with have reiterated the sentiment I had during my years in the trenches: How did I do it before? But reliance on the ever-increasing speed and capacity of these systems brings up another point—what happens if the system suddenly poops out?

Remember that you're still working with mechanical parts, parts that eventually wear out and will sooner or later break down, like your old reliable Chevy. Or your sheeter, or oven. And more than likely it'll happen between 5 and 8 p.m. on Friday night! To avert a catastrophe, follow these two steps:

1. Always have an emergency stash of blank paper order pads on hand, and

2. Periodically review manual order-taking procedures with your service people.

It is possible to run a store without an automated POS system, using paper order pads and pens and pencils. It's even possible to turn a profit. I've worked in both environments, raised by the manual method. I can still remember our spinning pinwheel used by the servers to clip orders on, as well as the consistent flow of mistake pizzas which were either discounted or thrown out. And the angry customers at the cash register who were charged incorrectly, the delivery customers on the phone for five minutes while orders were tabulated and a total price quoted. Not exactly conducive with high profits and efficiency.

But the day came when our little franchise was introduced to POS, and, after an awkward training period, we had "gone live". It wasn't long before we were looking behind us, wondering how we kept the customers coming back. We figured it must have been the food—because speed and efficiency wasn't afforded us by our order-taking system anyway.

Yet, there are many who avoid crossing that inevitable technology threshold for a variety of reasons, most orbiting around a fear of the unknown. I've heard a multitude of reasons for not going with "computers" in their shops, and then I've talked with some admittedly computer-illiterate people get hooked up and never look back. Keeping in mind that this book isn't selling any one product or way of doing business, I'm going to wade into some bold waters and tell you that without a powerful POS system, you're automatically out-served and out-produced by those with it.

Think of the ineligible handwriting that leads to mistake orders and lost revenue—gone with POS. How about the tickets that mysteriously turn up "missing" at the end of a shift, the ones probably leading to a paper trail of an inhouse thief—no more worries with POS. Yes, as with any system, there are loopholes, areas of susceptibility. No control system is invincible. But you sure cut down the chances of tampering with a computer tracking your traffic!

Systems: From Phones to the Makeline

But aside from controlling order system tampering, there's the customer service side. Advanced phone systems have smoothed the path in some cases for today's seamless integration of POS and pizza.

The pizza business is reliant on the telephone for communication (as are most other modern service-oriented businesses). Without the ability to call in orders, delivery and 99 percent of carryout would be non-existent. Long gone are the standard one- to three-line phone systems that could take a call at a time, leaving other callers with a busy signal. Now we have phone banks—even trunk lines at call center hubs—that integrate with a shop's local area network, which includes the POS stations and back office computers.

The future in POS is gearing for integrating with faster data transfer and faster processing speeds of incoming and outgoing data. Some systems send data to an in-house database, hard drives stored in the back office; others use application service providers (ASPs), or Web space on out-sourced servers, to store and maintain data. There are many options, depending on what you feel comfortable with.

The case for keeping your data in-house is that you know where it is, and you're able to archive whatever data you want and in whatever fashion you desire. Some opera-tors cringe when they consider a phone line going down that's leading to outsourced data banks or service provider, or a server crashing that's miles away, losing data en route and possibly some of what was stored. They also see order-taking abilities at a standstill until the outsourced company or ASP gets the system up and running again.

The case for storing and collecting data elsewhere is you pay someone else to maintain it, in their own space. Proponents point out that hard drives kept in the restaurant are subject to heat and dust, the causes of the feared CRASH. And even then, operators must call a geek to come fix it, paying an often hefty service call bill and waiting a while before it's up and running again. ASPs tout that geeks are in residence, and can hop on a problem as soon as it shows itself.

Both cases are legit, both cases have merit. The key is finding what a POS provider offers in terms of service in both emergency and routine situations. Is there a 24-hour help desk? Are there programmers on staff that can walk you through a difficult situation (i.e., lock-up, crash, power outage, etc.)? Remember that customers suffer (as do your sales, accordingly) the longer you're unable to take orders.

The impressive power of POS to integrate the entire order process, from the telephone call (or the server) with an incoming order to the makeline, then from the customer's door (or the table) to the cash register, then to the accounting, inventory and payroll arm of the system. It's all integrated to help you fulfill the needs of your customers and your employees, as well as maximize your operational management.

One advantage pointed out to me by an operator was the flexibility of his POS to send specific orders to specific stations. At this chain's stores, kitchens for dine-in orders were set up with a make station for pizza, one station for sandwiches, one for pasta orders, one for appetizers, one for soups, and one for baked entrees. The carryout/delivery kitchen was a mirror set-up, with as many stations. Needless to say, when the rush hit, there was a lot of zigging and zagging, which resulted in frequent bottlenecking and mistake orders.

After the POS was installed, the production time and the number of screwed-up orders dropped dramatically, as orders were split from a main ticket and routed to the appropriate stations. It all came together at the pick-up station, and customers, employees and managers were happy! The efficiencies gained with the automated ordering process also allowed the chain to remove an extra worker during some periods. Since a phone worker can take, say, double the orders with a faster order-taking system, why staff an extra person? The labor savings added up quickly.

Utilizing a call center is probably the apex of the efficiency of the marriage of telecommunications and digital data. One company rises from the dust in this regard, a company called oneSystem. Focusing on a one-number call center, where a region's customer base calls a single number for carryout or delivery, calls come into the center where the order is taken, and then routed to the appropriate location.

At these stores, the phone never rings. What you get is a totally integrated order-taking system, where data at all locations can be viewed as it happens, and in one place.

I visited one of oneSystem's call centers and witnessed the tremendous power of gathering information as it happened. As a district manager in charge of five units, for instance, if I see a location becoming overwhelmed with delivery business, I'm able to reallocate my resources and take care of the situation by dispatching drivers from another location. The communications streaming into the call center is considered a backbone, fully integrated with all the stores and able to disseminate information instantly.

Control Manually or Get E-nabled?

If increased customer service and streamlined systems aren't enough reason to grab onto a top-notch POS system, think of the headaches that will vanish if you do. I'm talking about the kind of headaches that recur, time and time again, simply because their source are part of managing a restaurant. I'm talking about administrative work.

The labor you used to put into administrative tasks like manually calculating and counting time cards is cut way back. (Did I hear some of you sigh with relief?) Although POS is an acronym for 'point of sale', the integration of these systems includes features that function as time clocks, for example. That's right—no more crossed eyes and throbbing temples at midnight trying to accurately crunch times-in and times-out.

This also goes for closing books, where accuracy is critical in cranking out reports used to make important decisions later.

Controlling your cash to the penny with each transaction has always been the elusive ideal for much of retail. This is one hot spot when figuring what your return on investment will equate to, and how long it'll take to pay off the purchase. Look at your cash overages and shortages, calculate out the gross difference from the ideal, or even amount (the beautiful '0'), in the last three years of business and you'll see how much you've missed a system like this.

Inventory control is another lifesaver. By tracking inventory the POS way, you're able to computerize the stocking and food-ordering process by ridding your shelves of slow-moving items and turning over stock faster. As for the labor involved in inventory, there's still a need for the physical count, but even as this book goes to press many operators are utilizing scanners.

In place of scribbling down numbers and using a hand calculator as you go, scanners read bar codes on most food items and the data goes directly into the POS system's inventory, or the data can be temporarily stored and downloaded into the system later.

A key inventory feature is deriving an ideal food cost. As an operator without a POS, I can recall spending an entire day every quarter performing the dreaded PCA (product cost analysis). The systems on the market today allow managers to keep in constant focus of their shops' variance from ideal food costs.

As pizzas and everything else on the menu are sold, the amount of ingredients which should have been used in preparation is tracked. While most operations conduct one- or two-week inventory counts, it's possible to do a count at any time and analyze the variance from ideal food cost at any given time. This is handy if you're tracking particular shifts or the proficiency of particular individuals. It's also an accurate judge of when product is 'disappearing', if that's an issue.

The more aware a crew is of the system's power and accuracy, the more likely food costs will come in line with the ideal and internal theft will lessen, if not cease. It's amazing to watch how well food costs are controlled when the people around the food are held accountable and become conscientious.

I personally know of pizza companies that have cut their ideal food cost variance by almost five percent after switching from manual to computerized.

The great thing about PCs being in more and more shops is that 10 years ago, having a computer inside a restaurant was virtually unheard of, especially in pizza restaurants. It seems that traditions are hard to break ... until the bottom line starts talking.

Having a local area network inside your four walls allows you not just control when you're there, but when you're away, too. The functionality that popularized the Internet is the same tool that makes POS so cool—with many systems you're able to "plug in" from wherever you are. And now, thanks to the blossoming world of wireless communications, you don't even need a modem nearby. Kick back in your boxers, coffee in hand, and see how the store did over the weekend!

Some POS providers offer a high-speed dedicated subscriber line (DSL) connection that links to reports generated over the Internet, where servers hold the data. All you need do is log on to a Web site and pick up whatever reports you need.

The Internet and Pizzeria Functionality

The Web and pizza work well together in terms of supply-chain management as well. What's been tagged 'e-procurement', getting supplies through cyberspace is the new up-and-coming way of doing business. And it's not just pizza. Business-to-business transactions is the catalyst of online growth, and is expected to surpass retail business on the 'Net soon.

The pizza industry has been slower to catch on than others, and from what operators and some large chain leaders have told me, it's the personal interaction they don't want to sacrifice for expediency. Conservative thinkers consider both the worst-case scenarios (running out of product and not having a person to call for an emergency delivery) and the day-to-day transactions. They ask, "How do I know an order went through? Am I getting the best prices when I can't haggle with a computer screen?"

But I predict it's just a matter of time before every pizza player will be hooked up with at least one distributor (chances are their largest). Other vendors are available to call on in case of unforeseen outages, and price checks are as simple as checking out the competing distributors. The phone will never go away. In fact, suppliers have told me that, despite popular belief of 'Net nay-sayers, instead of cutting sales staff due to going online to sell products, sales people will convert to more of a consultant/product expert role. More of a customer service specialist.

Some companies tout that ordering online can reduce costs by up to five percent because of the elimination of paper and other administrative fluff. Also, when an order is sent electronically, an operator's able to input an order at his or her leisure and send it the next morning or some other preset time. No more phone call interrupting you, no more time wasted giving an order, and even possibly having it read back. No more numbers written down incorrectly, and therefore less returns.

On the other end of the fiber optic, the Internet's role in pizza ordering is still to be fully realized. Although one online pizza portal claims that it'll handle $10 million of online pizza sales this year—up from a few thousand in '99—the vast majority of pizza lovers haven't utilized the Web to this end.

The big reason is due to an even quicker, easier way—the tried and true phone call. Even though companies are pushing to make the purchasing public realize that an online order avoids having to wait while on hold, allows for presetting a delivery or carryout order-ready time, and prevents mistakes when the order is taken, making that call is a hard habit to break. Is the public as interested as talking to a voice as some operators are with their suppliers? Seems the human element is a hard to one to shake.

But just like with the e-distributor issue, online ordering will likely increase, but never overtake traditional ways of conducting business. Aside from customers' slow grasp of Internet ordering, operators have found that technological advances have had a slow learning curve themselves.

Those inside the pizza industry have long awaited a seamless integration, where customers could surf the Web, place an order and POOF it arrives on the kitchen printer. The problem is that when a customer orders on a Web site, the order is usually sent to a central site, such as a call center, and a human being routes it to the correct pizzeria. That, or the order arrives from the Internet, directly to a store, and it's converted to a fax which is then used as the order ticket. Another method has been used that captures the Web order, sends it via phone call, and a digitized voice presents the order.

The issues many operators face is that it's difficult to find a reason to institute Web-ordering capability if a cost savings can't be realized. Most haven't jumped on the virtual storefront bandwagon because the demand isn't evident. With the above modes of order delivery, you're still using a person at one point or another, who requires pay for their efforts. To jump the cost-benefit hurdle, there would have to be an ordering blitz on the Web site to be a feasible option. This may not necessarily be true for the larger chains, which can make up for sluggish response to a site with sheer numbers of units.

That's not to say there haven't been some impressive steps toward a working model. The one-call company mentioned before, oneSystem, is working with the communications backbone already in place in its call center operations to support data routes from the Internet. I've seen a prototype Web site that allows customers to build a pizza and order it. After the order is placed, the data is routed on phone lines, just as any usual order would travel. The difference is, of course, there's no person taking the order over the phone at the call center—the data packet (the order) shoots straight to the appropriate store with no human interaction. That is, of course, until the cook at the make line rips the ticket from the printer.

There's also a push toward utilizing various technologies to order pizza, especially in the wireless world.

Motorola and Domino's recently tested wireless application protocol (WAP) on selected markets to see how things flowed. People were able to order pizza on their cell phones, by selecting a store, selecting from a complete menu, and even speed-ordering their last order if they wanted.

A company called Aloha, a POS provider, is also in the wireless fray, as are a smattering of other companies. Using WAP-enabled cell phones, this sort of technology is rumored to be the next big thing—but then, WAP was being stoked about five years ago, too.

Perhaps it took this long for all the other legs of the table to be in place, and for the rest of the technologies to catch up. This integration is called an L-Commerce Platform, standing for information that's 'location-based'. Using the location-referencing high-tech platform, consumers with cell phones, PDAs and pagers can place orders digitally—never by voice—to the nearest store wherever they are. Not only that, but maps are provided to lead customers to the shop. You're even able to pay before arriving to pick it up, or before the delivery driver meets you at your door!

For the business owner or manager, you're able to advertise to someone literally driving near your location. Stop and think about this: as Mom, Dad and little Susie drive home from a school function, tummies rumbling, their car approaches a present distance from your place. Dad's cell phone beeps, he picks it up, and what do you know—Joe's Pizza Shack has a $13.99 special! Where do you think they're more likely to stop for dinner?

Yes, pretty powerful stuff indeed.

Proponents of online ordering (I happen to be one of them, but I'm still hearing phones ringing off the hook) see that for those consumers whose habits are still being formed, it's just a matter of time before big percentages of business will come in from the Web. Not all the traditional core demographic of the 18 to 34 year-olds have formed the phone call habit; many more, year after year, are more comfortable with online interaction than talking on the phone. Another point to be made is that Internet connections are becoming faster. And a faster connection means the hassle of getting online (particularly on weekend nights when servers—the virtual kind—are busy) will eventually be nonexistent, and ordering online will be easier than by phone. Also, shops that have been receiving online orders for a while now report that they're able to charge a premium for Internet pies. The reason: Web shoppers are the more affluent group, and are apt to pay for convenience. Plus, operators realize that there's not much competition in cyberspace. For now anyway.

What You Can Expect to Pay

You'll rarely find your perfect POS systems and vendor on the first go-around. In a feature package I wrote not long ago for *Pizza Today,* focusing on all aspects of the latest POS systems on the market, every operator or chain buyer I spoke with was either on their second or third POS system. Something had gone sour somewhere along the line, or their old system didn't afford them some functionality they had hoped for. Since POS systems can run as much as the top pizzeria expense (ovens), it's wise to go out of your way to make an informed buying decision.

Know that with some POS providers, everything you purchase is from their company. This may include components, software, hardware, even phone equipment. One negative with such a setup is that when you're unhappy with, say, the software, you must either wait for the next upgrade or pay an arm and a leg for a techie's visit and manual upgrade. And you're usually trapped if you're suddenly disgruntled with service, since to throw out one part of the system means you must toss it all out and pay for another vendor. Plus, there's always some down time associated with big overhauls.

Costs are varied, but the range for a system with hardware, software, components and setup charges will run you $9,000 to $20,000, or even more depending on bells and whistles. Beware of those companies with a "lowest price guaranteed" sales pitch—there may be more under the covers than what you're seeing.

It's wise to think ahead when purchasing POS— don't just buy for your needs of today. Think where you're likely to be in five to 10 years. Ask probing questions like: how much volume will your store(s) be making; how many stores do you anticipate running? Key to planning ahead is installing POS that's able to be integrated later to keep up with evolving technology. The best systems I've seen are those with an open architecture, or one that's able to use multiple versions of different software packages—a sort of "plug-n-play" POS system.

Other factors to consider when pricing your total cost of POS ownership include printers and ink cartridges, software that comes with the system and what must be purchased separately, warranties, hardware upgrades, training and support.

Pizza Platitude #7

There are but two ways of rising in the world: either by one's own industry or profiting by the foolishness of others.

Jean de LaBruyere (1645 - 1696) French philosopher, writer

8

Paint Your Bottom Line Black

Yes, this book is about people. And pizza, of course. But come on, it's about money, too! Let me lead into this truism with one thought that may make you stand back with a concerned look on your face (at least I hope it does, at first anyway):

Pizza is a big-money venture, but it's not necessarily a big-profit one!

How can that be? Easy, if you don't have controls in place. You can score big in the sales column of your balance sheet, but the scales will tip at the end of each day toward loss if there aren't controls in place. And at the source of those controls are people--hey, it's that people thing again!

But people and profit go hand in hand; you can't have one without the other. This goes for every aspect of financial control. When you stop and think about the title 'Manager', what's the first definition that pops into your head? Look at the ones following and slam your finger down on the one you came up with.

A manager (man' i jer n.) is...

1. Someone that ensures product quality/consistency.
2. A person who is responsible for the efficiency of others.
3. Someone who controls the money in the till.

4. Anyone who is willing to work 60 hours a week and knows how to unlock and lock the doors.

Well, hopefully you didn't point to #4! But the others, well, they all apply, don't they? And they, along with many other functions and responsibilities, define what you and your supervisors really are: managers of everything! Let's get appallingly literal here. The English word 'manager' is derived from the root word 'man'. (I can hear you thinking, 'Hey, there's genius.')

But look from where 'man' originates—from the Latin 'manus' which means 'hand'. We get 'manacle' from the same definition! So, you can either think of the term 'manager' as someone having his hand in everything or on everything in your business, or someone who's shackled to the shop. Which one works for you?

That's the English lesson, now for the history lesson. Many moons ago, horse trainers used to practice with their horses in pacing. I live just across the Ohio River from Louisville, Kentucky, the horse-racing capital of the universe. In the surrounding area there's also a lot of horse farms and a lot of horse people. Just a lot of horse going around in general. When the Derby's on, and the horses are flaring nostrils and racing for the finish, you see pure talent and muscle in the horses, products of good breeding.

But when you watch an equestrian contest (a horse show), you're watching a whole heck of a lot of training. That's the pacing practice the trainers have instilled in the horses, time and time again, until they have it down perfect. This training is called practicing the manege, which was the front-runner for 'manage'.

So, when it literally gets down to it, managing is training (although I don't suggest running your people like horses).

And the goal of training is to paint your bottom line black. This includes training not just your servers

Counting the Cost: Inventory Safeguards and Strategy

Do you know exactly how much product inventory is in your shop right now? Or at least, do you know how to find out quickly and easily? If not, pull up a chair and let's talk.

You've probably heard it before, but it's worth repeating: losing track of your inventory is like losing control of the money in your cash till, or in your safe. If a case of cheese walks out your back door to feed a dorm room, you just lost some money—in essence, you've been robbed.

The retail world calls this shrinkage, which includes employee theft. It's so common that most retail chains allocate for shrinkage on their financial projections; in the books there's a line item for, say, a three-percent budget allocation for missing merchandise. Since that line's not on your books, it's in your best interest to track inventory levels frequently.

Other segments in the restaurant industry are exceptional examples of doing physical counts of inventory. I've heard reports that steakhouses will do from two to four steak counts every day. These places don't have a steak shrinkage problem.

Are you able to be so frequent and dedicated to counting inventory? Not a chance! Because of limited staff sizes, pizzerias can't do daily counts, unless on partial inventory. But a weekly count is a pretty good idea, especially if food costs are a bit out of line. Stores with consistently level food costs that are within budget can get by with conducting physical counts every other week or once a month. The point is: keep it consistent, whatever the time frame.

In regards to shrinkage, when employees witness management making a conscious and quite visible attempt to check what's on hand, the chances of theft are reduced drastically. Being sneaky just got tougher. Getting away with it suddenly became more task than fun.

Besides, how do you know what items are missing or are disappearing?

I talked with a man-and-wife team that had just opened their third shop. They decided to purchase a security camera system with multiple cameras in each store. The video feed from the cameras was accessible from their home computer, and they loved it because they could monitor the business as the day and evening passed. If one store needed help, they could shift employees and managers from one store to another—the ultimate labor allocation tool!

One day, the wife decided to play back the video from the night before after close. This had never been done, as the primary purpose was to check on the stores during opening hours. Much to her shock, she watched two trusted employees cook pizzas and drink beer with friends—three hours after close and on the house! Recalling more video from other nights the two employees closed together, she discovered that they had been going home with cases of ham, pepperoni and cheese, as well as other items.

Her comment to me was something like, "I knew food costs were kind of high, but I never would have suspected those two..."

And that's usually the situation; people you trust most take advantage of that freedom and ripe-for-the-picking environment. Don't get me wrong, there are plenty of trustworthy people out there. But to not have inventory controls in place because you're a trusting person is naive. When it comes to controlling the finances of your shop, it should be business first, personal second.

Counting your inventory not only gives you an accurate report of what's on your shelves, but it certainly gives you more control in terms of how much to order. The more frequent your count, the more accurate you'll identify trends and nail your incoming order. Keep in mind that you set the pace for the count. There's no need for waiting until next Monday to count—especially on those items you've noticed becoming out of line. Plus, a random count is sure to make potentially scheming employees think twice about lifting product.

Some operators rely on par levels (the quantity of an item needed on hand to make it through until the next delivery), but par levels actually distort actual food costs. And when there's bad information to base management decisions on, there's invariably going to be bad decisions made.

"But where will the time come from?" you ask. If you're not used to taking a physical inventory at regular intervals, time seems to be the enemy. Depending on the complexity of your menu and the size of your store, it may take six hours or more to count all you have. To speed up the process, make it a two-person job. This allows one person to count (meaning, counting those products as items—i.e., 4 cases, 228 boxes, etc.—or other appropriate quantity—i.e., 4.5 pounds, 4 quarts, etc.) while the other person writes on the count sheet. This can cut the time in half.

Other time-savers include:

๑ Recording on a standardized, up-to-date count sheet with items listed in the order you'll be counting;

๑ Organizing all the storage areas and ensuring items in their appropriate places;

๑ Counting on the slowest day of the week, and after either the lunch rush or the dinner rush;

๑ Having a calculator handy to add items and even begin ending inventory calculations as you go.

High Demands and Distributors

But before there's inventory to control, distribution channels are first carved out.

As an operator, you're charged with serving quality food. That quality comes first and foremost from your suppliers, who depend on the many food distributors to transport their product to your shop. Thus the reason this discussion of distributors is found in a chapter on controlling financial elements. Choosing and continuing to work with a good distributor is one variable you have almost complete control over. It's a lot like volleyball: as soon as you're playing on the receiving side of the net you turn around and serve what you get. In that regard, controlling what you receive is most certainly a controllable element in your business.

Simply put, distributors are the middle men of the food supply chain. They make it possible to deliver inventory to your back door, and usually at fair prices—often at discounted prices to keep your business. So intertwined is the relationship between operator and distributor, many on both sides consider it as much a part of life in the pizza business as breathing. Thus the importance of linking up with a good distributor.

When choosing a distributor, I once had asked Dennis Grocholski, director of operations for Figaro's Pizza, what he had used as a starting point. He listed what I consider an extremely thorough series of questions, one of the best I've heard of. Dennis suggests asking the following of a prospective distributor:

- Tell me about the diversity of your inventory. How many different packers or manufacturers do you represent for olives, canned tomato products, cheese, flour, and meats?
- How do you determine which lines you carry?
- What is your documented level of order fulfillment?
- What will you commit to provide to us in the way of order fulfillment rate?
- What is your policy and what are your proce dures to resolve orders that are delivered incoplete?
- What is your policy on minimum orders? If a unit falls below the minimum order, what are the consequences?
- Regarding delivery, are you able and willing to accept that our unit(s) can only accept deliveries between the hours of __a.m. and __a.m. and between __p.m. and ___p.m.?
- Do you offer a discount if I am willing to accept a key or night drop?
- Do you have "will call" capabilities? If yes, please explain the procedures.
- Are you utilizing state-of-the-art distribution

technology? Do you provide software that allows your customer to order via the Internet, at a time and date convenient to them? Can I see a demonstration of the software?

🚍 Do your delivery vehicles have onboard computers, so that you can track their progress and keep your customers informed if there is a problem? At what point and how do you notify customers if a delivery is running behind schedule?

🚍 If I choose to utilize a product not currently in your inventory, what required monthly or annual movement do you require before allowing slotting of new items?

🚍 What are you willing to do to assure me that the prices you are providing to me now are not merely lowball prices to buy my business?

🚍 What is the frequency of price changes?

🚍 Cheese is a major component of my food costs; how is your price for cheese determined?

🚍 What are your payment terms? What is the discount for early payment?

🚍 What is your policy on returns? How quickly can I expect a credit memo?

🚍 What can you tell me about the financial position of your distribution company?

🚍 Will you provide me a complete list of your current customers and those customers you've lost in the past year so I can check your references? (If not a complete list, can you provide me with a list of 20 current and 10 former customers?)

🚍 May I have a tour of your facility AND talk with employees as part of the visit?

After asking these questions, and getting adequate responses, you should be able to make a confident decision regarding who will be your distributor.

The main ingredient to forging a lasting relationship with a good distributor is trust, a word that comes into every conversation I have about distributors. So make sure that a sense of trust exists before signing any contractual agreements.

Food Costs, Portion Control and What They Have in Common

Supplies are delivered, inventory is accounted for, and food costs should be squared away ... except for one other major area of concern: portion control. Believe me—and all you pizza vets voice your agreement at any time—if your cooks aren't watching the specs, forget about controlling food costs.

I say this without abandon because of my experience. It is, however, the experience of some that portion control is for either the far-sighted or the ignorant. I've been in many shops (very successful mainstays of the community, may I add) where you'll never find a chart outlining specified topping quantities. When asked about how costs are kept in line, the common responses are something like: "Our cooks know what it should look like; they've got a feel for it—it's a handful; we don't need cups or scales slowing us down."

Well, okay, fine. I'm not there inspecting the place,

after all. Whatever works, fine. The pies do come out of the oven looking decent and tasting scrumptious, after all. But for the purposes of this chapter on controlling your cost, may I recommend setting some standards. Reason being, mainly, one guy's hand isn't the same size as another's—and very rarely will you employ the same tenured cook longer than one year. (May I also suggest for you operators out there with long-time, faithful cooks—reward them financially straight off the bottom line if your food costs are in line.)

There is plenty to say about using portion control to determine ideal food costs, product cost analysis, and other figures that help in running your operation—but we won't get into that here. Perhaps formulas and applications can be discussed further in another book; for now, let's stick with the importance of keeping an eye on controlling your costs through portioning.

Portion control extends, as does inventory and purchasing, over your entire operation: from the back-of-the-house dough prep in the morning to the sandwich maker at night; to the salad preppers in the wee hours to the waitress pouring drinks near closing; from sea to shining sea. Portion control also begins with setting standard portion sizes.

Ah, standards—the rules that govern our every move. Ever get caught speeding? You broke a standard, and lost money. Ever bounce a check? Your slip cost you even more cash. Same goes with those that try to scoot past food portion standard weights or other measurement, like cups, counts (28 pepperoni on a medium pie) or dimensions (1/4-inch cucumber slices for the salad bar, you get the picture). There are also standards for recipes: sauces, dough, dressings, etc. Let those standards slide and you end up paying eventually in a tightening profit margin.

Academically, standard portion size is defined as the quantity of an item that's served each and every time the item is ordered.

When you think about it, not only is your profit hampered on that product—enough to get you hot under the collar, but customers are also disadvantaged when they receive inconsistent product—enough to make you furious.

The paying public demands the same thing, over and over again. They expect what they're paying for, nothing more, and certainly nothing less. Yes, in my 11ish years in the trenches, I can vouch for many a manager that tilted the scales the other way in an effort to improve his or her food costs. Invariably it resulted in lost business, thus reduced sales, due to inconsistent product. Customers thought they were getting ripped off, a feeling that was verified when they ordered another time and received over-spec'd product. In a couple of cases I witnessed dramatic sales declines at these stores and lost jobs as a result.

Common tools are used to implement portion control: spoons, ladles, plastic cups, bowls, scales, slicing guards on knives or slicing equipment. There are even plastic rings which fit over the lip of pizza pans to control how far sauce is spread toward the outer rim (I've used these, and while messy during a rush, they help create a near-perfect sauce- and cheese-free crust).

Combined with thorough training up front, plenty of follow-up, and an easy-to-understand specification chart, portion control can be had. Laminated wall charts are great, as they'll resist everyday wear and tear, but always keep a new, clean chart on the premises. Change out the chart from time to time—even Superman can't see through six-month-old pizza sauce crusted over the ladle specs.

As I said before, there are those that'll never be caught using these items. Which, in my opinion, is okay-fine. That is, if the store is staffed with employees that have been around since creation and can, in fact, throw together near-identical pies time after time.

If you're struggling with turnover, or are opening more than one unit, or plan on operating in a region with historically high turnover, spec your product. Portion control is a must for simplified training and product consistency. It's difficult to discipline a young worker for an under- or over-topped pizza when there's not portion control in place.

Laboring for Efficient Payroll

Speaking of turnover, young help and overall pizzeria success, how many hands go up when I ask: "Who's hiring?" How about when I ask: "Who's hiring out of desperation?"

By 2010 there'll be 24 million more bodies in the United States (and you thought traffic was bad now!). That's great news for us pizza people. More population means more mouths to feed! But with the rising demand for pizza will come a steadily rising demand for workers to make and serve it. The market with 24 million additional people is anticipated to be served by one-third fewer workers.

And, as if that isn't enough to make us squeamish, a survey by the National Restaurant Association showed that nearly half of restaurateurs list qualified labor as a top concern. No wonder, in an industry with turnover rates of up to 150 percent. Last year Domino's neared the 140-percent mark, forcing the company to look at ways to change the tide.

The biggest challenge for the pizza professional today and for the foreseeable future is recruiting and retaining "keepers"—quality employees that will help your financial performance. How do they help you financially? Off the top, just staffing adequately is a big plus.

A recent MasterCard International Restaurant Survey revealed that of the top 10 reasons people select one restaurant over another, six deal with service, three with food and one with value. For the pizza-minded operator, this is a fairly monumental revelation.

Pizza, a product historically perceived as a value item, is no longer sought after for its price, but for the service surrounding it. And without people, of course, there's no service, or at least as many of the little extras that consumers now expect.

To succeed in the future, pizzeria operators must utilize what help they have in the most efficient way possible. Streamlining operations to maximize a store's labor efficiency is a strategy that will ultimately separate the sheep from the goats.

One method is using management systems, such as scheduling to an ideal sales (or volume) forecast. This can be done manually, but only after trends have been documented and forecasts are projected. Working backwards, you must first determine what your target labor cost percentage based on sales will be. Then, segmenting what sales are projected to be daily, and then by lunch and dinner on each day, you're able to determine how many people to schedule. I won't get into detail here, but would be happy to send a sample worksheet upon request.

There are also computerized management systems

that interface, or are an element of, today's advanced POS systems. In your store's database of number of orders and time segments, suggested schedules can be coupled with past schedules to give you a quick printout.

One of my happiest moments in management was the time when we were up and running with our first automated payroll system. I looked at my old rumpled schedule hanging on a nearby wall, penciled smudges and crossed-out shifts dotting the 7-day week, and chuckled inside. I considered running to it, ripping it down and disposing of it ceremoniously. But there were ladies present, and I thought better of it.

The other method of maximizing staff efficiency is leading. That's right, leading people. Here's where it's time to rise above the definition of managing and consider the true, deep-rooted meaning of an operator's life in pizza. That meaning is to lead people to be the best they can be under your leadership. That takes adhering to the standards and procedures you've set forth, and following through with helping them improve performance.

A waiter, even if with years of experience behind him at other restaurants, may be weak in up-selling. Help him improve that aspect of his job. A prep cook may have a tendency to overwork the dough—work with him to perfect his craft. It's leading people to a more efficient and proficient place in their jobs, not just managing to get from day to day.

One of the best slices of advice I can give to empower employees and give them a bit of ownership in the business is open book management. Opening your books for your employees to see, to visualize, the financial situation allows them to see the cause-and-effect relationships of their work. Most hourly employees—sadly, even some managers—don't know how the pizzeria sales dollar is divvied up. Their minds see money coming in the front door and think it's all going into the owners' and upper management's pockets.

Who's to lose when you give your employees a glimpse at your P&L? Photocopy balance sheets, line item costs like food costs and labor percentages, or anything else that matters, in the break room, in the kitchen. Chart your success, allow the employees to see how well they're doing.

Open book management is actually open book leadership—using this technique breaks any barriers of trust that may develop between one or many employees and management. An employee tends to think: "All right, I do count in this place. The big guy trusts me to make a difference, and I can see it." The result is an employee that puts forth more effort, completing the circle of trust.

Leadership in the pizza restaurant is essential to attracting and retaining the good ones out there. It's also important to lead by example (the old adage is true after all!), in that your actions in the things discussed about in this chapter are lived out. Remember that labor is the one most controllable expense. You and your managers are in direct control of it, which means keeping production moving when it's necessary, and spending the rest of your energy recruiting quality hands.

One secret I've learned in the quick-paced pizza biz is to never wait until you need the extra help—always hire before you need to. When you're not forced to cram interviews in awkward time slots and you don't feel pressured to get that extra body for next Friday night, it seems the good hires drift in unexpectedly. If your mind isn't pressed, the likelihood of making good hiring choices rises exponentially. Thinking along logical, clear lines of thought and solid strategy is just as important for what's going on outside the pizzeria.

A Tale of Two Marketing Strategies

When considering how to best market pizza, how large of a budget do you think is needed? What's surprising is that many successful pizzaiolos have reached profit pinnacles thanks to an advertising budget of ... nothing. I visited one store that had people lined up outside in the rain before they even opened their doors on their grand opening day—yet not one dime was spent on promotion.

This stands in contrast to other, seemingly bottomless advertising budgets, namely those of the big chains. Consider that Pizza Hut and Domino's combined to spend over $239.5 million in media expenditures in 2000.

The difference in marketing approaches isn't unique among modern business models: one comes from the repeated exposure and price point angle, the other from a reliance on old-fashioned word-of-mouth advertising. Both are effective, and there are plenty of points in-between, but the low-cost marketing I've witnessed in both small towns and metro downtowns is pretty extraordinary.

I've seen creative approaches like: hosting a pizza eating contest during special events, where media is invited; becoming a collecting point for things like aluminum can donations; collecting and matching donations for all sorts of worthy causes; providing pizza cards or coupons for local schools to sell for fundraisers; and the list goes on a mile. (For some free creative idea generators, visit www.pizzaprosperity.com.)

Low-cost marketing usually involves the investment of just time and product. The rewards that are reaped are new customers and long-term sales growth, something that's hard to put a finger on. Because of the difficulty of tracking from what promotion sales are drawn, old business models can't put the success on paper. But it works nevertheless. In most cases, this type of marketing involves doing something that's considered worthwhile for a community or a business or organization within the community, and then publicizing the daylights out of it.

Analyzing such marketing strategies from a cost-benefit perspective, it's a no-brainer—there's virtually no cost and plenty of benefit. Some people call this "local store marketing" or LSM, and the larger chains push unit managers to get involved in their communities in light of the obvious rewards. Some also tie in "good will marketing" with this strategy of low-cost marketing, believing that the more good you do the more business is generated. But this is only true for those that get the word out.

The difference between big ad budgets—involving direct mail couponing, TV, radio, etc.—and no-frills is that of how your name is thrust into the public's eye. What I've seen is a ton of free publicity, and it almost always circulates around a press release or a phone call to a few key media people.

Event tie-ins, such as the donation idea, are newsworthy enough to usually end up somewhere in the paper. And if you add the element of a well-known person in the community—WHAMMO, you may very well be found on the front page, or on the evening news. And what did it cost you monetarily? Nothing but the nickel you spent faxing over the release.

As an ongoing strategy, word-of-mouth spreads quickly. This sounds great, but keeps operators on their toes. Relying on word-of-mouth advertising means ensuring impeccable facilities, superb service and top-shelf quality. And that's all the time. One thing the big boys have going for them is deep pockets and the ability to saturate a market with advertising, which brings in a lot of product trial, regardless if a customer's last visit was so-so.

As I noted before, these approaches aren't anything new. But it's interesting in the world of pizza, because you see the two schools of thought regarding public perception of pizza and sales trends.

A Pennsylvania newspaper business editor e-mailed me recently inquiring: "What's the likelihood that Bertucci's will be able to grow into a national chain, as they're proposing to do, without growing too fast?" His follow-up question contemplated if there was any room for another national chain. My answers—as you can imagine, having read this much of the book—was a long one. (There's a lot to talk about when considering these sorts of questions!)

My answers dealt with the changing perception of pizza in our country. In both questions, I replied that Bertucci's is quite capable of becoming a national player, and do so without growing so fast as to lose focus on service, quality and consistency. And that's even with a fairly extensive menu with wood-fired pies.

Many pizza pros have learned from the mistakes of others who have grown just for the sake of growing, forgetting about the fundamentals. The results were lost customers, lost business, and the inability to enter markets years later. The public had been burned on poor quality and terrible experiences. So today you're seeing chains with eyes on expansion, yet with their hands on operations.

This leads us to the two schools of thought as it pertains to marketing in the pizza world: there are those consumers that hold on to the historic pizza perception of value and price; and there are those in the service and high-end quality camp. In the past, massive amounts of marketing dollars were spent only with the price-conscious in mind; now we're entering a new era where price doesn't matter as much as higher quality and caring service.

Some concepts are struggling through this transition period. These are the traditionally value-based locations, like the pizza buffets and the college campus-area delivery shop. While the delivery shop that sells $7.99 large one-toppings will no doubt be around forever—the captive college crowd will always be there, a market whose demand for cheap eats will never fade—the family-oriented locations face an uphill challenge. These concepts must somehow change their identity to keep up with an evolving public pizza perception. One example is CiCi's, a buffet concept that's gone to great lengths to change its image: a new logo, pizzas with fresh ingredients and more sauce and cheese, new décor to reflect a warmer feel, and even higher price points—it hadn't raised prices for 13 years.

Pizza Hut is also spending millions on interior upgrades to meet public perception, focusing more on its dine-in look and operation than its other revenue streams. California Pizza Kitchen recently dumped its plans to expand its CPK ASAP compact-version units for a roomier full-service version. More and more companies are catching on that it's not about speed and value as much as it is service and quality.

Just as there's the price-conscious consumer (a declining crowd), there's also the price-conscious (coupon-happy) operator. Business is indeed generated by pizza coupons for some, but not for everyone. As was mentioned in the section on labor cost control, consumers are now choosing one eating place over another by and large because of service and quality, not price or value perception. Of course, this rules out the obvious, such as the college student.

In short, if I were still in operations, I'd be excited about my marketing future. I could choose whether or not to direct mail, instead of be forced to because of price wars. I could exploit my product instead of cheapen it. And I could concentrate on selling to my immediate market, knowing that it's going to pay off in the long run.

Industry Highs, Lows, and Profit In Your Pocket

The fruit of controlling your variable expenses is that magic word: profit. I've often wondered (again, being a weird word guy) if the almost-spiritual lift of hitting your profit goals is the reason behind the word itself. Although I can't show this one to you in any dictionary, I'm guessing 'profit' is derived from those sages that passed on good news in ages past—the Prophets. A good word from a prophet meant good crops and less pestilence for the people—looks like they'd profit from that!

But when a Holy Man walked into town in sack-cloth, look out; trouble was a-comin'!

Interesting how the same connotations hit a pizzeria

operator when the writing's on the wall: "Profit's down". But what exactly are the profits like in the average pizza restaurant? Before I lay out some numbers, heed a little disclaimer: these ARE NOT in stone, true to every pizza restaurant in the world. Every operation, even the individual units within a chain, will always have different—and sometimes widely varied—cost percentages.

Why the painfully obvious disclaimer? Seems there was a sudden rash of IRS investigations, particularly in New Jersey, telescoping their sights on pizza restaurant operators not long ago. I began to receive phone calls from attorneys—not all from New Jersey, but all over—wanting to know what the industry standard was on certain line costs. The reason for their calls was a bit disturbing.

The IRS claims that operators have under-reported taxes stemming from under-reported sales for some time, and they could prove it by determining how many pizzas each shop makes a year. Then, of course, they wanted to know what usual costs were to determine what sort of profits were being made.

Thus the disclaimer. (If I knew some legalese, I'd throw it in for good measure, in hopes of staying out of a witness chair!) I say this in spite of the fact that a judgment was recently handed down disallowing the IRS from such practices; but you can't be too careful!

All that aside, and my butt covered, the pizza industry normally sees the following in a typical shop:

Food costs: 28-32%
Labor costs: 24-30%

Are you running too high a food cost if you're at 33%? No. Are you running too tight a ship if you're at a 22% labor mark? No. Not necessarily; again, it has to do with who you are, where you are, and what you're goals and budgets are.

Profit margins range anywhere from 0 to 20%, although the midrange (5-10%) is more common.

As you can see—and as you know, you pizza pros out there—your life as an operator could be the opening of any great novel, the verbiage depending on which direction the profit's going. "It was the best of times. It was the worst of times ..."

But as you'll see in the following section, the bad times made the tough tougher and the good times were just evidence of their success in pizza.

Pizza Platitude #8

Entrepreneurial profit . . .
is the expression of the value
of what the entrepreneur contributes
to production.

Joseph A. Schumpeter (1883 - 1950) Moravian-US
economist, sociologist
"The Theory of Economic Development," ch. 4,
1934.

9

Profiles in Pizza

The American Dream to many has dissolved with the prosperity found in the post-WWII states, or even with the chasing of far-away land found in the Wild West. This dream chasing equates to chasing after the wind for most, an ideology lost generations ago, along with identity and vision, the stuff of our founding fathers and other great men and women.

But without getting overtly philosophical (oops, too late!), there is hope found in these elements borne in most Americans, the desire to grab onto our heritage of risk-taking and to ultimately stand atop the world with our trophy in hand. Why else does competitive sport continue to thrive? Go to any high school athletic event and watch those in the stands—parents, teachers, students; they're as enthusiastic about winning as the kids on the court!

So what of this long-lost American Dream and the need among us to win? It can be shown that sports are in another arena than business. But are they truly on different playing fields when it comes to our innate want of The Title, The Blue Ribbon, The Plaque? My take is that in the world of pizza anyway, where I sit in a front row bleacher seat, they are indeed one and the same—and it's the stuff champions are made of!

My life in pizza thus far has brought me into contact with some pretty exciting people, from dynamic independent operators with their own styles that make them special, and the heads of the largest pizza companies on Earth. I could write a book just highlighting the stories behind their individual and corporate successes, tales that brings smiles and occasionally a jolt of empathy. (Who knows, that may be the next edition out!)

They each have caught the fox of a dream after the thrilling chase, their stories each are lit with the light of inspiration that shine on what we Americans share. Some paths began in pizza and ended in other glorious pursuits; some began in another industry and ended in pizza. However varied the journey, their feet have all tread the path of success. And for the aspiring pizzaiolo, what finer path is there than to follow their examples, share their experiences, and learn from their mistakes.

Small Independents That Wear Big Pants

When I say 'small', I'm thinking in relative terms when compared with other players with many locations. And when business decisions are made in light of the fact that their store is only one in over 63,000 in the country, it takes a huge heart, enormous will and tremendous staying power to come out on top.

Dominic Tedesco (we'll call him Nick, since we're all friends) is one of those guys kids look at and want to hug—he's just got that demeanor. Owner of Tedesco's Authentic Italian Pizzeria in Jeffersonville, Indiana, Nick's story is one that makes you sit up and take notice. He grew up "in the business", helping out in his parents' Italian restaurant in

Louisville, Kentucky, and now at 37 he's been running his own shop for four years. Going back to his upbringing explains his passion for "real" pizza.

Both of Nick's parents are Italian: his father from Calabria and his mother from Sicily. Dad was captured by American soldiers in WWII, and was sent to the states as a prisoner of war. After Mussolini was killed, the elder Tedesco had a choice of becoming a U.S. soldier in Italy and finish out his term or stay in America. He chose to stay, and met Nick's mother later (she arrived via Ellis Island). Nick's older brothers were born in Italy, after the couple were married in the homeland, and Nick was born in the states.

What at one time surely looked bleak for the future of a Tedesco family tree, what with a war going on and Dad caught in the middle, a seed of the love of food and gatherings became the passion that light's Nick's fire today. Nick's father went right to work in restaurants as soon as he was a free man, and that's the hook that caught Nick. The southern Italy flare for spice is a favorite of Nick's, and he uses it whenever he can on his menu, which is now given out at a second location in nearby New Albany, Indiana. And he's intending to grow even more. Two new locations are pending as of this printing.

Billy Lane's roots may not stem back to the southern tip of Italy, but he's got some Southern in his voice just the same. Born in Sumter, South Carolina in 1942, Lane would never forget the days of his childhood, as he intended one day to recreate the era. And he has, in his own 4,500-square-foot full-service shop called Pizza Lane. Everything from old gas pumps to a wooden cigar-store Indian grace the walls of the place. Lane was a Pizza Inn franchisee in Shreveport, Louisiana for 20 years (in with his uncle, one of the first Pizza Inn players) before missing Sumter so much he moved back and opened Pizza Lane.

Steady sales are attributed to the fact that he's doing business in his hometown. Success is measured by repeat customers, as he knows he's on track when customers he's had for over 20 years are still coming back, and so are their kids. It's not been all rosey: one attempt at opening a second location in another town failed, and he recalls when pizzas were half the price they are today and higher profit was realized—a testament to increased overhead and other costs.

But that hasn't stopped his creativity. Lane has recently begun selling parbaked pizzas to grocery stores and private schools, with tremendous success. With the private schools, the pies are catered in, or as he noted, making good on "high class delivery as we call it in the South." Lane's in for the long haul, as he's as comfortable with his first-name-basis clientele as they are with him.

Three guys from New York decided one day that Staten Island needed a quality pizza to call its own, and from there, Goodfella's Brick Oven Pizza was conceived. While waiting in line outside a pizza joint before it opened at 2 p.m. in New York City, E. Jay Myers and his two brothers-in-law asked another customer what his reason was for braving the New York City traffic—having driven from Staten Island himself—only to wait in line for 40 mintues for a pizza. The customer told them it was worth it, plus there was a need on the island for a quality pie.

The three guys pooled together $75,000, and went to work after their day job (like Myers' management position with a cosmetics company) and worked often til 3 a.m. to get up and running. The big effort went toward a homemade brick oven, smack in the middle of the dining room.

The first Goodfella's opened in '93, and at the time of printing there were five locations in New York and 11 more planned.

The fellas at Goodfella's hold an incredible 20 to 24% profit margin with the help of an average $20,000 per week in sales. Here's an example of the desire to make quality product, even without any previous pizza experience. Yes, you can be taught! In fact, Goodfella's was ranked "Number one pizza in America" in '94 and '95 by Pizza & Pasta, and New York mayor Rudolph Guiliani has been noted wagering their pies as bets with other mayors during Yankees' playoff games.

The last independent is a woman whose success in the midst of adversity is truly an inspiration, if not for other women, for any operator who thinks they've got it the toughest. Mary Ann Rouse, owner of Bill's Pizza & Pub in Mundelein, Illinois, started making and serving pizza in her parents' pizza place when she was 13 years old.

The business grew into a highly successful and well-known northern Illinois destination. Several years later, Rouse developed a recipe and production schedule for Bill's frozen pizza line, which is now sold in schools, grocery stores and even several bars. Her next venture was opening Bill's Pizza & Pub in September of 1999, and is now averaging over $1 million in annual sales, selling over 1,000 pies each Friday night.

What's so unusual about all this? She's a single mom, raising two sons on her own through it all. They're older now and help her in the new restaurant, and may now be able to relate to the long hours she's had to put in over the years. After 28 years in the industry, her story is one that inspires and paints a picture of the quintessential indy.

Mid-level Chains Making News

Equipped with only $500, a rented storeroom and some equipment from a Pittsburgh scrap yard, Jim Fox finally grabbed hold of his dream of owning his own pizza shop. More than 220 stores and millions of pizzas and sandwiches later, Fox's Pizza Den celebrated its 30th anniversary in 2001.

Fox started making pizzas when he was 12 in a little shop in Monroeville, Pennsylvania, a day when a large plain pizza cost 75 cents. Pursuing his dream after high school, Fox opened a shop in his hometown of Pitcairn, Pennsylvania, in 1971, selling out of everything on that first night by 10 p.m.—300 pizzas in six hours.

Times, tastes and economics have changed since the '70s, but Fox's Pizza Den has rolled with the changes, taken a proactive stance and blazed its own trail instead of following one. One such instance was Fox's home delivery—before delivery was popular. And it didn't start with a fleet of vehicles and brightly lit signs on the roofs of vehicles. Fox bought an old VW van, built a wooden delivery box with shelves in the back of the van and painted the vehicle with Fox's colors and logo. Heat-containing delivery pouches were unknown in 1973. Instead, Fox daily cured hot bricks from a local mill and placed them in the bottom of the box to keep the pizzas warm.

Franchising is a concept that Fox's Pizza Den has taken to heart, and its application of the concept to business has yielded an 18-state network with more than 220 locations. Fox financed his first 15 stores personally, using his home as collateral each time. Once the business community saw that his concept worked, he established relationships with two major lending institutions in Pittsburgh to provide financing for franchises.

Fox has another goal in mind when establishing franchises: He prefers to set up stores in smaller towns, where both the owner-operator and the community at large can benefit.

For would-be entrepreneurs in small towns, there's a lower overhead and lower investment to get involved in the franchise. More than 20 percent of Fox's franchise owners are people who started working in the chain and progressed to owning franchises. Success magazine recently named Fox's as number two of all pizza franchises on the basis of franchise owners' satisfaction.

Along with implementing his franchising plan, Fox established the Fox's Pizza Commissary, Inc., in 1986, which enables franchise owners to conveniently order top quality food products and have them delivered to their stores. Fox hired professional wholesalers to help in managing the commissary, and since its inception, the commissary staff and its sales have more than tripled.

With 30 years behind him, Fox says things are only going to get bigger. Annual sales topped $60 million last year, and Fox's Pizza Distribution, Inc. provides franchises with products that enable the company's 1,950 employees to sell more than 6 million pizzas and 5 million sandwiches per year.

Today, Fox's Pizza Den is ranked among the top 20 pizza companies in the world by Pizza Today. It has won numerous awards, such as being named best pizza franchise in 1993 by the National Pizza and Pasta Association, a 1986 Italian award for best sauce and Fox's own honor of being named a finalist in the Western Pennsylvania Entrepreneur of the Year awards.

Fox's is currently growing at an annual clip of 40-50 stores. The summer 2000 issue of Pizza Marketing Quarterly magazine ranked Fox's Pizza Den ninth on a list of the fastest-growing chains in the country.

In the same region of the country, another success story was brewing around the same time. When Jim Grote was a sophomore at Ohio State University in 1963, he borrowed $1,300 from his father (who, at the time, thought pizza was just a fad) and future father-in-law to purchase a little neighborhood pizzeria in Columbus, Ohio. Grote decided to drop out of college to devote his time and energy to the place. In Donatos Pizza's infancy, Jim and his mother hand-mixed the dough at home due to the tight confines of the kitchen; Jim's father, who was a butcher, created a unique sausage recipe that's still used in company stores.

Donatos grew steadily, opening new locations in and around Columbus, and began franchising in 1991. Looking for franchisees to help grow the brand, yet doing so at a careful pace, Grote was approached by foodservice giant McDonald's in May of '99 with a surprising offer: the burger gods were looking favorably on the 143-unit pizza chain and wanted in. It seemed everybody was shocked, even Grote. Suddenly Donatos had enough financial backing to take the chain national, if not global.

Grote remains an integral presence in operations, and three of his kids are also on board with executive positions—all part of the deal. While some would be content to jump ship with the loot, Grote's standards and passion for pizza keeps him at it. Donatos story is an exciting one to say the least. My first thought when the 'McDonatos' news hit the streets was that it's an enormous feather in the caps of pizzeria operators everywhere—big and small—to think that the world's largest foodservice company would latch onto pizza (and a regional chain at that) as an important segment of their overall operational growth.

Two years have passed since the initial news of the merger, and we're yet to see exponential growth for Donatos. And that's even more encouraging to see, I think. I see Jim Grote wise enough to maintain his standards and procedural intelligence in regards to pizza, and resist rushing in.

I predict that Donatos is going to help McDonald's in two major areas: further penetrating the U.S. market, since the burger segment has nearly reached saturation; and leading the charge into the mega company's interest in technologically advanced ordering platforms, namely online ordering. (Another reason I'm keeping my eye on that front!)

The latest report is that they plan to open 25 stores a year, mostly in the Southeast and Midwest. At the time of printing, Donatos had 164 stores.

Another college kid started a company, but this one much more recently. L. Scott Granneman began East of Chicago operations in 1990, and, like Donatos, began franchising in '91. Granneman surrounded himself with those he trusted, college buddies—most are still helping run the show in some pretty nice offices in Willard, Ohio, where they're headquartered. Growth was always in the plan for Granneman (who developed his own deep pan crust recipe early on); the group of friends are doing something right, as they're currently running over 125 locations.

East of Chicago is planning on continued expansion

of a rate of 30-40 stores this year, mainly through franchising, and will undoubtedly be seen as a force to be reckoned with in new markets soon.

Speaking of rapid growth, another mid-level chain that's making a huge splash is Papa Murphy's Take 'n' Bake Pizza based in Vancouver, Washington. So phenomenal is their growth and unique their way of doing business, Pizza Today chose the company as the premier Chain of the Year in 2001. Terry Collins founded Papa Murphy's in 1981, after running a deli.

Although the idea of take-n-bake pizza isn't new, Papa Murphy's remains the only pizza company that does only take-n-bake. Other companies, such as 114-unit Figaro's Italian Kitchen out of Salem, Oregon, and 15-store Nick-n-Willy's from Boulder, Colorado, also cook pizza, giving customers an option. (It's interesting to note that these companies are all based in the West; take-n-bake appears to many living in the eastern third of the U.S. as a new concept. It's just taken this long for it to reach the rest of us!)

The absence of cooking ability allows for trim labor budgets as well as reduced start-up costs, both of which contribute to the company's rapid growth. Papa Murphy's is second only to Papa John's in terms of real growth, and may lead all expanding companies this year. There were 617 locations at year's end 2000, 117 more than '99, with $260 million in sales. Executives are estimating at least another 100 units will be added in 2001.

Big Chains and How They Got So Big

In the pizza world, you'll often here about the "Big

Four". These are the four largest pizza chains, after which the number of units and sales volume drop considerably (see the Top 25 Pizza Chains in the back). The Big Four consists of Pizza Hut, Domino's, Papa John's and Little Caesars.

Through the middle of the '90s, the Big Four were expanding, kicking butts out of markets, taking no prisoners. But as the decade ended, various dynamics adversely played into each of the companies and slowed growth; business dynamics like forced closures of under-performing units and lack of consumer confidence.

Even Papa John's, on an incredible roll for such a long time, announced in late 2000 that same-store sales had dropped in the first fiscal quarters of the year. Domino's is now resigned to single-digit growth, as market watchers have seen with Pizza Hut for some time. But then, any growth is good growth; it just wasn't as intense these past five or six years.

Partly to blame was 2000's bottoming out of cheese prices, which, when combined with the then-current discounted pizza-price wars, virtually obliterated store comp sales. Little Caesars closed over 300 units in 1999 alone; Pizza Hut's U.S. market share dropped almost $250 million in the last decade.

Stock prices for both Pizza Hut and Papa John's are still struggling after the legal wrangling between the two companies, Pizza Hut's at about half its '99 value and Papa John's is in about the same shape. Wall Street analysts are obviously skeptical about either company's ability to crank out sales and profit growth as they had in years past.

When you step back from the picture, however, and use your imagination as a time machine, you see many of the same stressors on the shoulders of the young men that created the companies. When you contemplate where they began and how far they've brought their dreams, the cyclical patterns of business and negative impact all fades away. Somehow you just know their companies are going to bounce back (you even wonder if they would have survived the stock market crash and the Great Depression!). In particular, let's look at two of them: Tom Monaghan and John Schnatter.

Monaghan was born in 1937 in Ann Arbor, Michigan. His father died four years later, ushering in a childhood of foster homes and orphanages. Years later, in 1960, while attending the University of Michigan, Monaghan and his brother James borrowed $900 and bought a small pizza store called DomiNick's in Ypsilanti, Michigan. In less than a year Monaghan bought his brother's share of the business and formed another partnership, opening additional stores in Ann Arbor and Mt. Pleasant, Michigan.

The story behind Domino's and the many obstacles Monaghan conquered throughout the years, and the path he took to success was compiled for the first time in his 1986 biography, "Pizza Tiger".

He pioneered several innovations in the pizza industry that have set standards among other operators, such developing dough trays, the corrugated pizza box, insulated bags to transport pizzas, the pizza screen, a conveyor oven and a unique franchise system enabling managers and supervisors to become franchisees.

In December of '98, after running the company for 38 years, Monaghan sold Domino's to Bain Capital in order to devote his attention to his non-profit activities. He still remains on the Board of Advisors in an advisory role. Monaghan founded Legatus, an organization of Catholic business leaders, in 1987 after receiving an inspirational meeting with Pope John Paul II.

The founder of Papa John's, John Schnatter, is still calling the shots in Louisville, Kentucky. Since he knocked out a broom closet in his father's Jeffersonville, Indiana pub, sold his '72 Z28 Camaro to buy $1,600 worth of used equipment and started selling pizza to the pub patrons in 1984, Schnatter's not looked back. In 16 short years, he's managed to grow Papa John's to the third largest pizza chain the world.

After he attained his business degree from Ball State University, friends laughed at him when he shared his dreams of franchising five to six stores a month. Without pause, Schnatter was soon selling 300 to 400 pies a week out of the converted broom closet.

The first Papa John's opened in '85 and the first franchised unit happened in '86. Eight years later, Business Week put Papa John's at the summit of its Hottest Growth Companies, and Inc. gave Schnatter's new pizza company a 51st spot on its 100 Fastest Growing Small Public Companies. The next year, Forbes recognized Papa John's as number 10 on its Best 200 Small Companies in America. That same year, the company was ranked first in Entrepreneur's pizza category and 34th overall in its Franchise 500 Listing of the best franchise opportunities in the U.S.

By the mid-90s, Papa John's nudged up to the number four placement on Pizza Today's Hot 100 Companies. Schnatter will credit his company's success to the people put in place around him, but without his tenacity and positivism, I'd venture to guess it wouldn't have made it this far, this fast, this successfully.

An element that Schnatter has brought to the table that hadn't existed before, at least in such scale, is the central commissary system of supplies. As locations are franchised out, and operations begin, a regional commissary distributes fresh dough balls. Such expediency has led to consistent product laced with quality, something unseen in the delivery realm circa 1985.

One interesting note: Frank Carney, who founded Pizza Hut with his brother Dan in 1958, had left Pizza Hut to pursue other ventures. Come to find out, his heart was still in pizza, and knowing a good product when he saw it, he suited up with the Papa John's team. Now he's a franchisee with what would have normally been challenging competition.

There are thousands of stories like these in the world of pizza. I'd like to hear yours. Send me a line, either via e-mail (tracy@pizzaprosperity.com) or snail mail (Tracy Powell, 2405 Kingsfield St., Jeffersonville, IN 47130).

Let me know your story (the 'why' and the 'how' concerning your life in pizza), along with financial data such as sales. In future editions, I intend to publish more intriguing insights into the people behind the pizza!

Pizza Platitude #9

*A pessimist sees the difficulty
in every opportunity;
an optimist sees the opportunity
in every difficulty.*

Sir Winston Churchill

Status of the Pizza Industry

* Unless otherwise noted, statistics and analysis are from studies conducted by either Leading Edge Reports, the National Association of Pizza Operators, or Empowered Innovations.

Overall restaurant industry sales are forecasted to reach $399 billion in 2001, an increase of 5.2% over 2000. Of this, pizza restaurant sales are expected to reach $27.5 billion, a 5% increase over 2000. At the time of this printing, there were 63,575 pizzerias in the U.S., an increase of 1,280 units over last year (a 2% growth). Pizza restaurants make up 7.5% of the nation's total 844,000 restaurants.

Total pizza industry sales was $28.889 billion at year's end 1999, segmented into pizza restaurant sales ($25.523 billion) and packaged sales, or, frozen and deli sales ($3.366 billion).

Total sales are projected to exceed $33 billion by 2003. This will be a 17.2% growth rate, constituting a sales increase of more than $4 billion. Pizza restaurant sales hold an 88% share of the total pizza market, and alone is projected to grow by 16.5% and is expected to exceed $29 billion in sales by 2003.

␣␣␣

Pizza restaurant breakdown in 1998, with sales of $25.097B:
* Chains $15.8B
* Independents $8.9B
* Institutions $397M

Pizza restaurant breakdown projection for 2003, $29.248B:
* Chains $18.379B
* Independents $10.383B
* Institutions $486M

    Shares of pizza restaurant sales held by the market's three segments (chains, independents and institutions) have wavered over the past 10 years. Despite a prosperous decade in the 1980s, chain shares dropped to 61% of retail pizza sales by 1989. Chain market share did rise to 64.8% in 1993, but it slid slightly to 63.0% five years later.

    Independent pizza operators held a 37.5% share in 1989, but watched their share drop 2 points to 35.4% in 1998.

    Institutions saw their sales rise at a respectable rate during the 1980s, but market share remained fixed at 1.4% through 1996. Two years later, however, institutional shares had climbed to 1.7% of the total market.

Analysis from Leading Edge Reports

                         ✦ ✦ ✦

Mid-2000 U.S. market share in pizza sales:
· Pizza Hut, 18%
· Dominos, 9%
· Little Caesar's, 5%
· Papa John's, 5%
· Rest of Pizza Today's Top 100 chains, 20% *
· Independents and all other chains, 53% *

Mid-2000 U.S. market share in number of units (62,525):
- · Pizza Hut, 12.9%
- · Dominos, 7.4%
- · Little Caesar's, 5.9%
- · Papa John's, 5%
- · Rest of Pizza Today's Top 100 chains, 10% *
- · Independents and all other chains, 61.8% *

* Estimated with 1999 Top 100 listings

Change in U.S. market share trend, 1992-1998:

Who makes the best pizza?
According to a 2000 poll conducted by Zogby in which 1,202 U.S. adults were asked "If you had to choose one national pizza chain as makers of the best pizza, which would you choose?", respondents chose:

1. Pizza Hut, 39.5%
2. Papa John's, 19.8%
3. Dominos, 13.6%
4. Little Caesar's, 6.6%
5. Donatos, 1.4%
6. Other, 10.2%
7. Not sure, 8.8%

🢒 🢒 🢒

Consumer demographics
  ✎ 30% of pizza orders are from kids under 18
  ✎ The primary pizza consumer age group is the 18-34 year-old

✎ Pizza is the #1 food consumed at dinner time, up from #5 in 1990

✎ Fast food segment share by user type in 1999 was:

Burger, 45%

Pizza, 19%

Regional chains, 14%

Mexican, 8%

Sandwich, 7%

Chicken, 7%

🖋 🖋 🖋

Carryout and delivery:

In 2000, pizza consumers used carryout 42.1% of the time (compared to an all-QSR average of 32.6%); ordered delivery 36.2% of the time (all-QSR average of 8.9%); ate in the restaurant 20.5% of the time (all-QSR average of 30.7%); and used drive-thru 1.2% of the time (all-QSR average of 27.7%).

A 2000 study conducted by Sandelman & Assoc. showed that:

✎ pizza was the delivery food of choice for 90.9% of 600 fast-food customers;

✎ delivery is more often a group dining decision: only 7.8% liked eating alone, 47.1% of delivery customers would rather dine with a spouse, 38.9% with their children, and 23.5% with friends;

✎ the per-person check average for delivery purchases is higher than any other occasion: $4.72 vs. $3.93;

✎ delivery patrons are more likely to use a limited-time special, making such a decision 45.8% of the time. They usually learned about the promotion from direct mail fliers (46.7%) or newspapers (26.4%);

✎ compared to all-occasion beverage sales, where 69.7% of patrons ordered a drink with their meal, only 33.8% did so with delivery;

✎ the majority of delivery customers were white males, between 25 and 34 years old, married, with a household income of $50,000-74,000.

🖋 🖋 🖋

General Industry Info

* The June 19, 2000, issue of *BrandWeek* reported on the top brands in terms of media expenditures, listing Pizza Hut ($125.5M) and Dominos ($114M) in the QSR category. Pizza Hut was listed as America's 27th top brand, and Dominos ranked 34th.
* Pizzerias represent 17% of all restaurants.
* Of 33,617 pizza franchise units in the United States, roughly 73% (24,381 stores) offer delivery, 81% (27,129 stores) offer takeout, and 51% (17,082 stores) offer dine-in service.

🖋 🖋 🖋

Here are some fun facts culled by *Pizza Today* in the past:

* Ninety-three percent of Americans eat at least one pizza per month. (source: Bolla wines)

* Two thirds of Americans order pizza for a casual evening with friends. (source: Bolla wines)
* Americans eat approximately 100 acres of pizza a day.
* According to the National Restaurant Association, Italian ranks as the most popular ethnic food in America.
* According to a Gallup poll, kids ages 3–11 prefer pizza over all other food groups for dinner.
* Parade Magazine estimates that 94% of the U.S. population eats pizza.
* Approximately 3 billion pizzas are sold in the U.S. each year.
* If given the choice, 25% of Americans would prefer to share a pizza with Tom Cruise; 21% with Bill Clinton, 20% with Robert Redford, 13% with Sharon Stone and 13% with Cindy Crawford. (source: Bolla wines)
* Pizza ties with hamburgers (at 26 percent) at the top of the list of foods Americans cannot give up. (source: Bolla wines)
* Regular thin pizza crust is still the most popular crust, prefered by 61% of the population. Thick crust and deep dish tied for second, at 14%. Only 11% of the population prefers extra thin. (Source: CREST (Consumer Reports on Eating Share Trends), 1994)
* In 1994, fast food pizza restaurants captured one in five fast-food restaurant orders. (source: CREST)
* Part of pizza's rising popularity is its convenience for take-and-go eaters. In 1994, seven in 10 orders at fast-food pizza restaurants were consumed off the premises. Delivery orders from pizza restaurants represented nearly one-thrid of all off-premises traffic that same year. (source: CREST).
* The use of promotion is higher at pizza restaurants than at other restaurant concepts. IN 1994, more than half of all eater occasions at fast food pizza restuarants involved some kind of promotion. (source: CREST)
* In 1994, nearly three-quarters of orders at pizza restaurants were at

dinnertime and more than half of all orders occured on Friday or Saturday. (source: CREST)

* Pizza is no longer simply a late-night snack food: only three percent of pizza orders at fast-food restaurants were for an evening snack in 1994, down from six percent in 1990. (source: CREST)

* From 1990 to 1994, pizza orders rose 12%. (source: NRA)

* Pizza was ordered on 14 percent of all orders in 1994, up one percent from 1990. (source: NRA)

* Pizza eaters are more loyal than other fast-food consumers; 48% frequent only one restaurant chain. Chicken and burger eaters are more fickle, with only 39% of chicken choosers and 25% of burger buyers remaining loyal to one chain. (source: ADVO, Inc.)

History

* Pizza originated in Italy in pre-refrigerator times. Its most direct ancestor was "Casa de nanza", which means "take out before". Housewives would pound out dough into a thin crust and place leftovers on to bake. Pizza was a peasant food designed to be eaten without utensils and, like the French crepe and the Mexican taco, was a way to make use of fresh produce available locally and to get rid of leftovers. Because tomatoes were thought to be poisonous, the early pizzas didn't feature the tomato sauce common today. However, Columbus brought a new variety of tomatoes back to Italy from the West Indies that overcame those fears and thrived in the Mediterranean climate.

* The modern-day tomato-and-cheese pizza didn't come along until 1889, when Italian tavern owner Don Raffaele Esposito developed a pie bearing the colors of the Italian flag with mozzarella, tomatoes and basil.

U.S. Market Saturation Report

State	Total # Restaurants	# Pizza Restaurants	People per Pizza Rest.
Alabama	6440	554	8027
Alaska	1401	161	3894
Arizona	8267	870	5897
Arkansas	4025	495	5400
California	58,734	5587	6063
Colorado	8945	899	4784
Connecticut	6660	1164	2926
Delaware	1513	254	3085
D.C.	1592	82 .	6976
Florida	25,742	5352	5352
Georgia	12,570	1124	7283
Hawaii	2794	165	7343
Idaho	2643	301	4299
Illinois	22,760	2976	4173
Indiana	10,968	1742	3491
Iowa	6184	1085	2697
Kansas	5181	596	4511
Kentucky	5972	858	4711
Louisiana	6674	546	8185
Maine	532	2396	2396
Maryland	8588	1025	5167
Massachusetts	14,015	2235	2841
Michigan	17,491	2972	3344
Minnesota	8834	1189	4137
Mississippi	3505	322	8834
Missouri	9928	1232	4542
Montana	2625	255	3538
Nebraska	3615	379	4515
Nevada	388	388	5150
New Hampshire	2534	471	2624
New Jersey	16,084	2648	3178
New Mexico	3098	325	559

U.S. Market Saturation Report (cont.)

State	Total # Restaurants	# Pizza Restaurants	People per Pizza Rest.
New York	36,305	5264	3605
N. Carolina	13,258	1482	5431
N. Dakota	1559	183	3037
Ohio	21,271	3738	3037
Oklahoma	6011	592	5829
Oregon	7322	797	4293
Pennsylvania	23,056	4619	2659
Rhode Island	2424	348	3012
S. Carolina	7038	696	5764
S. Dakota	1767	205	3682
Tennessee	8578	932	6104
Texas	32,113	2626	7940
Utah	3358	447	4996
Vermont	1408	190	3204
Virginia	11,338	1323	5350
Washington	12,123	1084	5437
W. Virginia	2960	539	3355
Wisconsin	11,759	1327	4042
Wyoming	1219	129	3828
Total		65,575	Avg: 4427

It's interesting to note the two extremes of American saturation: there are more pizza restaurants per capita in New England in aggregate (i.e., Maine, 2396 people per pizzeria; New Hampshire, 2624; Pennsylvania, 2659; Massachusetts, 2841), and less pizza restaurants per capita in the Deep South (i.e., Mississippi has 8834 people per pizzeria; Louisiana, 8185; Alabama, 8027; Georgia, 7283).

Of course, many factors come into play, such as regional economic viability, but certain areas can be targeted in the less saturated regions, particularly around the hot markets like Atlanta (which grew almost 40% from 1990 to 2000), the Auburn-Opelika, Alabama region (which has grown 32%), and New Orleans (although population growth is flat, per capita income is rising at a 9% clip).

Alphabetical Resource Listings

A

Agro Dutch Industries Ltd.
Phone: (770) 850-0063
Fax: (770) 951 2302
ifn@bellsouth.net
Fresh-packed Mushrooms

Atlas Cold Storage
5255 Yonge St., Suite 900
Toronto, Ontario M2N 5P8
Contact Mary Tibando
Phone: (416) 512-2352

B

Bowman Displays
648 Progress Ave.
Munster, IN 46321
PHONE (800) 922-9250
FAX (219) 922-8329
menuboards, stock food photography,
lightboxes, banners and much more!

C

CAMPUS COLLECTION T-
SHIRTS
P.O. BOX 2904
TUSCALOOSA, AL 35403
PHONE: (800) 289-8744
FAX: (205) 758-0678
WWW.CAMPUSCOLLECTION.NET
E-MAIL:
INFO@CAMPUSCOLLECTION.NET
T-SHIRT DESIGN/PRODUCTION
SCREEN-PRINTED/EMBROIDERED-
ITEMS FOR STAFFING, PROMOTIONAL,
RETAIL SALES
Consultants:
American Institute of Baking
Banis Restaurant Design
"Big Dave" Ostrander
Bruno & Associates
Buy Gitomer, Inc.

Carol A. Hacker & Associates
Center for Foodservice Education
Chart Your Course International
Correll Consulting
Foodservice Consultants
    Society International
Franchise Consulting Service
GEC Consultants, Inc.
GHR Training Solutions
Graham Communications, Inc.
Hire Tough Group
Karen Susman and Associates
Linda Lipsky Restaurant
    Consultants, Inc.
Out East Consultants
Rigsbee Enterprises, Inc.

CYPLEX, INCORPORATED
3255 CAHUENGA BLVD. WEST
LOS ANGELES, CA 90068-1375
(323) 436-0880
ALLIANCE POS SYSTEMS FOR PIZZA

D

DOLE PACKAGED FOODS
One Dole Drive
Westlake Villiage, CA 91362
(818) 874-4000
www.dole.com

E

Escalon Premiere Brands
Phone: 1-888-ESCALON
www.Escalon.net
Fresh-packed California Tomato
Products. 6IN1; Bonta; Bella Rossa;
Allegro; Christina's

ExactTarget
141 Green Meadows Drive, Ste. Three
Greenfield, IN 46140
(317) 467-4486
Info@ExactTarget.com
E-mail Marketing Services

F

FIDELITY COMMUNICATIONS
CORP.
41252 VINCENTI CT.
NOVI, MI 48375
(800) 683-5600
FAX: (248) 426-8580
E-MAIL: RICKS@FIDELITYCOM.COM
WWW.FIDELITYCOM.COM
WWW.WELLHELPYOU.COM
LEADER IN PIZZA STORE TELECOMMU-
NICATIONS. SOLUTIONS AT NATIONAL
ACCOUNT DISCOUNTS. OFFERING THE
NEW CALLWORKS ANSWERING SOLU-
TION. SERVICE 24/7.

Furman Foods, Inc.
P.O. Box 500
Northumberland, PA 17857-0500
phone: (800) 952-1111
fax: (570) 473-7367
www.furmanos.com
Furman Foods offers custom pizza and
marinara sauce formulations

G

Grote Company
1160 Gahanna Parkway
Blacklick, OH 43004
(614) 868-8414
Fax: (614) 863-1647
E-mail: sales@grotecompany.com
www.grotecompany.com
Sauce application & slicing equipment.

Innings Telecom Inc.
Innings Telecom Inc. is the developer of
CallWorks, the incoming call management solution that is quickly becoming
the telecommunications standard of
pizza operators. The product ensures
efficient order taking, increases profits
and enhances customer service.
CallWorks is distributed in partnership

by Fidelity Communications Corporation.
Call Innings at 800-363-4223, or visit
Innings' Web site at www.innings.com.

INTERNATIONAL PLAY COMPANY
Phone: (604) 607-5544
E-mail: ipc@direct.ca
www.internationalplayco.com
We design, manufacture, and install
children's soft-modular playground
equipment for both indoor & outdoor
applications. Call today for your free
design proposal.

K

KRISP-IT
15 E. Palatine Rd.
Prospect Heights, IL 60070
800-574-7748 (KRISP-IT)
Fax: (847) 808-8878
Keeps pizzas crisp for take-home and
delivery!

M

Marquez Brothers International
5801 Rue Ferrari
San Jose, CA 95138-1857
Phone: (408) 960-2700
Fax: (408) 960-3213
E-mail: mmancuso@marquezbrothers.com
Web site: www.marquezbrothers.com

Marsal & Sons
181 E. Hoffman Ave.
Lindenhurst, NY 11757
Phone: (631) 226-6688
Fax: (631) 226-6890
E-mail: marsalsons@aol.com
www.marsalsons.com
Brick-lined, gas-fired pizza ovens and
deck ovens

Microworks POS Solutions, Inc.

PrISM™ OneTouch, POS Systems
Designed for the Pizza Business
Call or Download a *Free Demo* today!
800-787-2068 x120 or **716-787-1090 x120**
Call Tim x120 ... **www.microworks.com**

Millennium Custom Foods, Inc.

3800 North Wilke Road
Arlington Heights, IL 60004-1267
Phone: (847) 259-8311
Fax: (847) 259-8312
E-mail: wingalos@aol.com
Finger Foods manufacturer featuring such
unique items as: Wingalos-Boneless
Wings, StuffSkins, Blossom Fryz, Zappers-
Stuffed Jalapenos and Keggers-Beer
Battered Onion Rings

MinuteMailer.com

395 McDonough Parkway
McDonough, GA 30253
E-mail: sales@minutemailer.com
www.minutemailer.com
MinuteMailer.com can design, print, carrier
route sort, and deliver the mailers directly
to your local post office ready for delivery.
They also have the technology to pinpoint
your BEST customers using state-of-the-art
geo-positioning technology, based on the
location of your restaurant. Then for subse-
quent ad campaigns it is a simple matter of
going on-line to change the offer and the
dates.

Mizell & Associates, Inc.

107 Marine Drive
Edenton, NC 27932
Phone: 888-749-9237
Fax: 252-482-1999
New & used pizza equipment
www.pizzaequip.com

Moving Targets

812 Chestnut St.
Perkasie, PA 18944
(800) 926-2451
**Affordable new-resident mailings. No
minimum! No contract! No set-up fees!**

N
National Marketing, Inc.

33975 Autry St.
Livonia, MI 48150
(734) 266-2222
Fax: (734) 266-2121
www.nminc.com
Smallwares, Delivery Items, Thermal Bags

O
oneSystem

1187 Coast Village Rd., Suite 1-151
Santa Barbara, CA 93108
Phone: (805) 965-7007
Fax: (413) 793-7190
**The pizza call center experts—one num-
ber call center software with fully integrated store-side POS.**
tellmemore@onesystem.com
gsmaldon@onesystem.com

P
PALAZZOLO MFG. CO.

743 BARG SALT RUN RD.
CINCINNATI, OH 45244
PHONE: 800-513-6333
FAX: 513-528-7016
CHEESE GRATER/SHREDDERS

R
Red Gold, Inc.

P.O. Box 83
Elwood, IN 46036
Phone: (765) 754-7527
Fax: (765) 754-3230
**Tomatoes & Tomato Products;
REDPACK, TERESA, etc.**

S

Safe-Strap Co., Inc.
10 Kingsbridge Road
Fairfield, NJ 07004
Toll Free: 800-448-8945
Fax: 973-575-8424
E-mail: sscoinc@aol.com
Manufacturer of Diaper-Depot Changing Stations, Child Protection Compartment Seats and Diaper Vending Machines for Restrooms.

Selbysoft, Inc.
8326 Woodland Ave. E.
Puyallup, WA 98371
Phone: 800-454-4434
Fax: 253-770-2997
E-mail: sp1@selbysoft.com
www.selbysoft.com
Touch Screen POS

SUGARDALE FOODS
PO BOX 8440
600 HARMONT AVE. NE
CANTON, OH 44711
800) 860-6777
SLAUGHTER@FRESHMARK.COM

Sun Roma Golden Tomatoes
Vine-ripened & ready-to-use golden Roma tomatoes. Choose from whole peeled, diced, strips and puree. No. 10 cans and 8-oz. cans available. Call sales at (877) 77-7691 for more information.

Vulcan-Hart Company
PO Box 696
Louisville, KY 40201
Phone: (502) 778-2791
www.vulcanhart.com

W

Warren Frozen Foods
Portioned or bulk pre-blanched pastas, lasagna sheets and strips, cheese-filled products. Contact Jan Larson at:
(515) 967-4254 ext. 221 or e-mail jlarson@auntvi.com

Z

ZEPCO DISPLAYS
LIGHTED & NON-LIGHTED MENU BOARDS. FREE LAYOUT
CONTACT—JOANN PLOTT
1-800-852-8412
www.zepcodisplays.com

Consultants

American Institute of Baking
Tom Lehmann, director, bakery assistance
1213 Bakers Way, PO Box 3999
Manhattan, KS 66505-3999
(785) 537-4750
(785) 537-1493 Fax
tlehmann@aibonline.org

Banis Restaurant Design
Tom Banis
PO Box 5542
Walnut Creek, CA 94596
(925) 934-1212
Facility design and layout

"Big Dave" Ostrander, "The Pizza Doctor" (c)
2152 East Bissonette
Oscoda, MI 48750
(888) BIG DAVE
(517) 739-9115 Fax
bigdave@voyager.net
www.bigdaveostrander.com
Marketing, customer service, cost controls, employee retention strategies

Bruno & Associates
Pasquale "Pat" Bruno
920 N. Franklin St., Ste. 201
Chicago, IL 60610
(312) 951-8102
(312) 951-8066 Fax
pasbruno@aol.com
Food preparation and presentation, operations

Buy Gitomer, Inc.
Jeffrey Gitomer
310 Arlington Ave., Loft #329
Charlotte, NC 28203
(800) 242-5388
(704) 333-1011 Fax
salesman@gitomer.com
www.gitomer.com
Customer service, sales management

Carol A. Hacker & Associates
209 Cutty Sark Way
Alpharetta, GA 30005
(770) 410-0517
(770) 667-9801 Fax
carolahacker@hotmail.com
Human resource management

Center for Foodservice Education
Jim Laube, CPA Restaurant
    Consulting Group
9801 Westheimer, Ste. 302
Houston, TX 77042
(888) 233-3555
(713) 783-0896 Fax
cfe@restaurantowner.com
www.restaurantowner.com
Profitability, financial management, staff development

Chart Your Course International
Gregory P. Smith
2814 Hwy. 212, SW
Conyers, GA 30094
(800) 821-2487

(770) 760-0581 Fax
greg@chartcourse.com
www.chartcourse.com

Correll Consulting
John Correll
8459 Holly Drive
Canton, MI 48187
(734) 455-5830
Kitchen design and layout, operations

Foodservice Consultants
    Society International
304 W. Liberty St., Ste. 201
Louisville, KY 40202-3068
(502) 583-3783
(502) 589-3602 Fax
fcsi@fcsi.org
www.fcsi.org

Franchise Consulting Service
48 South Service Rd., Ste. 1
Melville, NY 11747
(631) 465-2022

GEC Consultants, Inc.
Lloyd M. Gordon, president
4604 Birchwood Ave.
Skokie, IL 60076-3835
(847) 674-6310
(847) 674-3946 Fax
lgordon@enteract.com
www.gecconsultants.com
Site appraisals, feasibility studies, construction planning, business plans and pro formas, marketing strategies

GHR Training Solutions
Sheryl & Don Grimme
(954) 720-1512
solutions@ghr-training.com
www.ghr-training.com
Workplace violence; employee retention; teambuilding; stress reduction

Graham Communications, Inc.
John Graham, president
40 Oval Rd.
Quincy, MA 02170
(617) 328-0069
(617) 471-1504 Fax
j_graham@grahamcomm.com
www.grahamcomm.com
Market planning, advertising, media planning, public relations, research and analysis

Hire Tough Group
Mel Kleiman
8300 Bissonnet, Suite 490
Houston, TX 77074-9781
(713) 771-2818 ext. 119
(713) 771-0501 Fax
mkleiman@hiretough.com
www.hiretough.com

Karen Susman and Associates
Karen Susman
3352 South Magnaolia Street
Denver, CO 80224
(888) 678-8818
(303) 756-2687 Fax
kdsus@aol.com

Linda Lipsky Restaurant Consultants, Inc.
Linda Lipsky, principal
216 Foxcroft Rd.
Broomall, PA 19008
(610) 325-FOOD
(610) 325-3FAX
lipsky@restaurantconsult.com
www.restaurantconsult.com
Operations evaluations, server and cus-tomer service training, menu engineering

Out East Consultants
Bob Steiner, principal
42 Perry St., Ste. 3A
New York, NY 10014
(877) 568-8327

(208) 279-1088 Fax
solutions@outeastconsultants.com
www.outeastconsultants.com
Feasibility studies, start-ups, cost control, marketing, mystery shopper reports

Rigsbee Enterprises, Inc.
Ed Rigsbee
P.O. Box 6425
Westlake Village, CA 91359
(800) 839-1520
(805) 371-4631 Fax
edrigsbee@aol.com
www.rigsbee.com

Pizza Companies

Apparel
Campus Collection T-shirts

Appetizers
Millennium Foods
Sugardale

Baby-changing Stations
Safestrap

Bacon
Sugardale Foods

Call Centers
oneSystem

Computerized Mgmt. Systems
Cyplex
Microworks
Selbysoft

Direct Mail
ExactTarget
MinuteMailer
Moving Targets

Full-service Distributors
Presto Foods

Dough Additives
Krisp-It

E-mail Marketing
ExactTarget

Food Prep Equipment
Grote Co.
Mizell & Associates
National Marketing
Palazzolo Mfg.

Ham
Sugardale Foods

Ingredients
Agro Dutch
Dole
Escalon
Furman Foods, Inc.
Marquez Bros.
Presto Foods
Red Gold, Inc.
Sugardale Foods
Sun Roma

Marketing
ExactTarget
MinuteMailer
Moving Targets

Menu Boards
Bowman Displays
Zepco Displays

Mushrooms
Agro Dutch
Ovens
Marsal & Sons
Vulcan-Hart

Pasta
Warren Frozen Foods

Pepperoni
Sugardale Foods

Photographic Displays
Bowman Displays
Zepco Displays

Pineapple
Dole

Playgrounds
International Play Co.

Point-of-sale Systems
Cyplex
Microworks
oneSystem
Selbysoft

Refrigerated Equipment
Atlas Cold Storage
Palazzolo Mfg.

Sauce
Escalon
Furman Foods, Inc.
Red Gold, Inc.
Sun Roma

Signs
Bowman Displays
Zepco Displays

Telephone Systems & Service
Fidelity Communications
Innings Telecom

Toppings
Dole
Furman Foods
Agro Dutch
Marquez Bros.
Presto Foods
Sugardale

Franchise Legal References

The following firms are either specialists in franchising or have teams which specialize in the area, some to a greater extent than others. Many handle clients in multiple states outside their home office. Percentages represent percent of practice devoted to franchising.

Alschuler Grossman Stein &
  Kahan LLP
2049 Century Park East,
39th Floor
Los Angeles, CA 90067
(310) 277-1226
(310) 552-552-6077 Fax
Susan Grueneberg, partner
Direct line: (310) 551-9104
sgrueneberg@agsk.com
www.agsk.com

Arent Fox Kintner Plotkin & Kahn,
  PLLC
1050 Connecticut Ave., NW
Washington, D.C. 20036
(202) 857-6065
(202) 857-6395 Fax
Michael M. Eaton
www.arentfox.com

Armstrong Teasdale LLP
2345 Grand Blvd., Ste. 2000
Kansas City, MO 64108
(816) 221-3420
(816) 221-0786 Fax
Edward R. Spalty, managing
  attorney
Direct line: (816) 221-3420
  ext. 5208
espalty@armstrongteasdale.com
www.ArmstrongTeasdale.com
5-10%

Baker, Donelson, Bearman &
  Caldwell, P.C.
900 South Gay St., Ste. 2200
Knoxville, TN 37902
(865) 549-7000
(865) 525-8569 Fax
Kelli L. Thompson, chair: franchise
litigation secretary
Direct line: (865) 549-7205
www.bakerdonelson.com

Balch & Bingham LLP
2 Dexter Ave.
Montgomery, AL 36104
(334) 834-6500
(334) 269-3115 Fax
Robin G. Laurie, partner
Direct line: (334) 269-3146
rlaurie@balch.com
www.balch.com

Ballard Spahr Andrews &
  Ingersoll, LLP
1101 Laurel Oak Rd., Ste. 100
Voorhees, NJ 08043
(856) 627-8555
(856) 627-1153 Fax
Edward J. DeMarco, Jr., partner
demarco@ballardspahr.com
www.ballardspahr.com

Bartko, Zankel, Tarrant & Miller
900 Front St., Ste. 300
San Francisco, CA 94111
(415) 956-1900
(415) 956-1152 Fax
Charlie G. Miller, shareholder
www.bztm.com
9%

Bell, Richardson, Smith &
Callahan, P.A.
116 South Jefferson St.
Huntsville, AL 35801
(256) 533-1421
(256) 536-8995 Fax
James H. Richardson
jhr@bellrich.com
www.bellrich.com
20%

Blackwell Sanders Peper Martin
LLP
2300 Main St., Ste. 1100
Kansas City, MO 64108
(816) 983-8000
(816) 983-8080 Fax
Donald A. Culp, partner
Direct line: (816) 983-8115
dculp@bspmlaw.com
www.bspmlaw.com

Michael F. Brady
2118 West 120th St.
Leawood, KS 66209-0468
(913) 696-0466
(913) 696-0468 Fax
mikebrady@mindspring.com
100%

Buchanan Ingersoll Professional
Corporation
301 Grant St.
One Oxford Centre, Floor 20
Pittsburgh, PA 15219
(412) 562-8800
(412) 562-1041 Fax
Arthur J. Pressman, co-chair of
franchising group
Direct line: (215) 665-3910
www.bipc.com

Bundy & Morrill, Inc., P.S.
12351 Lake City Way NE,
Ste. 202
Seattle, WA 98125-5437
(206) 367-4640
(425) 984-7240 Fax
Howard E. Bundy
www.bundymorrill.com
100%

Burch Porter & Johnson
130 North Court Square
Memphis, TN 38103
(901) 524-5000
(901) 524-5186 Fax
Ralph B. Lake
Direct line: (901) 524-5186
10%

Carmen D. Caruso, P.C.
10 South LaSalle St., Ste. 3500
Chicago, IL 60603
(312) 920-0160
(312) 920-0162 Fax
Carmen D. Caruso
cdcaruso@msn.com

Carter & Tani
402 E. Roosevelt Rd., Ste. 206
Wheaton, IL 60187
(630) 668-2135
(630) 668-9009 Fax
Doris Carter, partner
cartani@cartertani.com
100%

Cassels Pouliot Douglas Noriega
1135 Rene-Levesque Blvd. W.,
Floor 31
Montreal, Quebec
Canada H3B 3S6
Anne-Marie Gauthier

Direct line: (514) 871-5402
www.pouliotmercure.com
7%

Clayman, Markowitz, Tapper &
    Baram, LLC
3 Regency Drive
Bloomfield, CT 06002
(860) 242-2221
(860) 286-0185 Fax
Judith A. Geery
cmth@earthlink.net
www.ctattys.com
10%

Dady & Garner, P.A.
4000 IDS Center
80 South Eighth St.
Minneapolis, MN 55402
(612) 359-9000
(612) 359-3507 Fax
Jeffery S. Haff, managing partner
Direct line: (612) 359-3505
mdady@dadygarner.com
www.dadygarner.com
100%

Kenneth F. Darrow, P.A.
9400 S. Dadeland Blvd. PH5
Miami, FL 33156
(305) 670-8200
(305) 670-2048 Fax
35%

Gerard P. Davey, PLC
550 Town Center Dr., Ste. 600
Santa Ana, CA 92705
(714) 434-9100
(714) 434-9111 Fax
daveylaw@msn.com
100%

Davis, Graham & Stubbs LLP
370 17th St., Ste. 4700
Denver, CO 80202
(303) 892-9400
(303) 893-1379 Fax
Thomas P. Johnson, partner
Direct line: (303) 892-7487
www.dgslaw.com

Fennemore Craig
3003 N. Central Ave., Ste. 2600
Phoenix, AZ 85012
(602) 916-5000
(602) 916-5592 Fax
Anne L. Kleindienst, director
Direct line: (602) 916-5392
akleindi@fclaw.com
www.fennemore-craig.com

Fisher Schumacher & Zucker LLC
121 Ave. of the Arts, Ste. 1200
Philadelphia, PA 19107
(215) 545-5200
(215) 545-8313 Fax
Lane Fisher, partner
www.franchise-lawfirm.com
100%

Flamm, Boroff & Bacine, P.C.
925 Harvest Dr., Ste. 220
Blue Bell, PA 19422
(215) 239-6030
(215) 239-6060 Fax
Harris J. Chernow, chairman: franchise law dept.
www.flammlaw.com
25%

Foley & Lardner
2029 Century Park East, Ste. 3500
Los Angeles, CA 90067

(310) 277-2223
(310) 557-8475 Fax
Mitchell Shapiro, partner
Direct line: (310) 975-7938
mshapiro@foleylaw.com
www.foleylardner.com

Franchise Law Team
30021 Tomas, Ste. 260
Rancho Santa Margarita, CA
92688
(949) 459-7474
(949) 459-7772 Fax
Cheryl Briggs, paralegal
www.franchiselawteam.com
100%

Friedman Rosenwasser &
  Goldbaum, PA
5355 Town Center Rd., Ste. 801
Boca Raton, FL
(561) 395-5511
(561) 368-9274 Fax
Ronald N. Rosenwasser, partner
Frost & Jacobs, LLP
201 East Fifth St., Ste. 2501
Cincinnati, OH 45202
(513) 651-6800
(513) 651-6981 Fax
Michael J. O'Grady
Direct line: (531) 651-6482
www.frojac.com
30%

Gibbons, Del Deo, Dolan,
  Griffinger & Vecchione
One Riverfront Plaza
Neward, NJ 07102
(973) 596-4500
(973) 639-6258 Fax
H. John Schank, II, partner: franchise practice group
Direct line: (973) 596-4809

jschank@gibbonslaw.com
www.gibbonslaw.com

Goodman and Carr
200 King St. W, Ste. 2300
Toronto, Ontario
Canada M5H 3W5
(416) 595-2300
(416) 595-0567 Fax
Sheldon Disenhouse, partner
Direct line: (416) 595-2354
sdisenhouse@goodmancarr.com
www.goodmancarr.com

Gowling Lafleur Henderson
2300-1055 Dunsmuir St. Box 49122
Vancouver, B.C.
Canada V7X 1J1
(604) 683-6498
(604) 683-3558 Fax
Leonard H. Polsky, partner
polsky1@gowlings.com
www.gowlings.com

Greenberg Traurig, LLP
One W. Camelback Rd., Ste. 1100
Phoenix, AZ 85012
(602) 263-2300
(602) 263-2350 Fax
Jeffrey H. Wolf, shareholder
Direct line: (602) 263-2434
www.gtlaw.com
75%

Gregory J. Ellis & Associates, Ltd.
999 Plaza Drive, Ste. 777
Schaumberg, IL 60173
(847) 413-0999
(847) 413-0959 Fax
Greg_EllisEsq@aol.com
90%

Greiner, Gallagher & Cavanaugh, LLC
2001 Route 46, Ste. 202
Parsippany, NJ 07054
(973) 335-7400
(973) 335-8018 Fax
Timothy R. Greiner
tgreiner@greinergallagherlaw.com
50%

Hahn Loeser & Parks LLP
3300 BP Tower
2000 Public Square
Cleveland, OH 44114-2301
(216) 621-0150
(216) 241-2824 Fax
Arthur M. Kaufman, partner
Direct line: (216) 274-2263
amkaufman@hahnlaw.com
www.hahnlaw.com

Hall & Evans, LLC
1200 Seventeenth St., Ste. 1700
Denver, CO 80202
(303) 628-3300
(303) 628-3368 Fax
John E. Bolmer, II
Direct line: (303) 628-3366
bolmerj@hallevans.com
www.hallevans.com

Head, Johnson & Kachigian
228 W. 17th Place
Tulsa, OK 74119
(918) 587-2000
(918) 584-1718 Fax
Rachel Blue, shareholder
blue@hjkklaw.com
www.hjklaw.com
10%

Hogan & Hartson, LLP
555 13th St., NW
Washington, D.C. 20004
(202) 637-5655
(202) 637-5910 Fax
John F. Dienelt, partner
jfdienelt@hhlaw.com
www.hhlaw.com

Hunton & Williams
951 E. Byrd St.
Riverfront Plaza, East Tower
Richmond, VA 23219
(804) 788-7212
(804) 788-8218 Fax
Michael J. Lockerby, partner
mlockerby@hunton.com
www.hunton.com
90%

Ice Miller Donadio & Ryan
one American Sq., Box 82001
Indianapolis, IN 46282
(317) 236-2100
(317) 236-2219 Fax
James L. Petersen, partner
Direct line: (317) 236-2308
petersen@imdr.com
www.icemiller.com

Jenkens & Gilchrist
Fountain Place
1445 Ross Avenue, Ste. 3200
Dallas, TX 75202
(214) 855-4500
(214) 855-4300 Fax
Joyce Mazero, franchise & distribution law practice group leader
Direct line: (214) 855-4793

Kanouse & Walker, PA
2255 Glades Rd.
One Boca Place, Ste. 324 Atrium
Boca Raton, FL 33431
(561) 451-8090
(561) 451-8089 Fax
Keith J. Kanouse, president
keith@kanouse.com
www.kanouse.com
50%

Kaufman & Canoles, PC
PO Box 3037
Norfolk, VA 23514-3037
(757) 624-3000
(757) 624-3169 Fax
Stephen E. Story
Direct line: (757) 624-3257
sestory@kaufcan.com
www.kaufmanandcanoles.com

Kaufmann, Feiner, Yarmin, Gildin
  & Robbins LLP
777 Third Ave., 24th Floor
New York, NY 10017
(212) 755-3100
(212) 755-3174 Fax
David J. Kaufmann, partner
Direct line: (212) 705-0810
dkaufmann@kfygr.com
60%

Harold L. Kestenbaum, P.C.
585 Stewart Ave.
Garden City, NY 11530
(576) 745-0099
(576) 745-0293 Fax
www.franchiseatty.com
100%

Erwin J. Keup
3015 Country Club Drive
Costa Mesa, CA 92626

(714) 751-3921
(714) 751-9321 Fax
ekeup@ca.freei.net
100%

Kilpatrick Stockton, LLP
1100 Peachtree St., Ste. 2800
Atlanta, GA 30309-4530
(404) 815-6800
(404) 815-6555 Fax
Rupert M. Barkoff
Direct line: (404) 815-6366
rbarkoff@kilstock.com
www.kilstock.com
95%

Mark J. Klein, P.C.
Commerce Tower, Ste. 2201
Kansas City, MO 64105
(816) 474-6137
(816) 478-2113 Fax
mjk@abanet.org
www.lawyers.com

Krass Monroe, PA
1650 West 82 St., Ste. 1100
Minneapolis, MN 55431-1147
(952) 885-5999
(952) 885-5969 Fax
Dennis Monroe, shareholder &
chairman
Direct line: (952) 885-5962
www.krassmonroe.com
30%

Law & Legal Management Office
of Kat Tidd, P.C.
14232 Marsh Lane, Ste. 75001
Addison, TX 75001
(972) 247-6934
(972) 247-7535 Fax
www.lawyers.com/franchiselawyer
60%

Law Office of Don M. Drysdale
610 Newport Center Dr., Ste. 700
Newport Beach, CA 92666-6498
(949) 760-9677
(949) 760-9551 Fax
www.donmdrysdale.com
90%

Law Office of Joel D. Rosen
1000 Germantown Pike, Unit B-8
Plymouth Meeting, PA 19462
(610) 940-1617
(610) 940-4376 Fax
imlawman@aol.com
www.lawyers.com/joelrosen
50%

Law Offices of Todd E. Stockwell
861 Corporate Dr., Ste. 201
Lexington, KY 40503
(859) 223-3400
(859) 224-1399 Fax
Elizabeth R. Kessler
erkessler@msn.com
30%

Law Offices of Van Elmore
500 17th St., Ste. 950 South
Denver, CO 80202-5402
(303) 659-7342
(303) 659-1051 Fax
vel@rmi.net
100%

Maddin, Hauser, Wartell, Roth,
  Heller & Pesses, PC
Third Floor Essex Centre
28400 Northwestern Highway, PO
Box 215
Southfield, MI 48037
(248) 354-4030
(248) 354-1422 Fax

Stuart M. Bordman
Direct line: (248) 827-1870
smb@maddinhauser.com
www.maddinhauser.com

Markus Cohen Law Office
22 St. Clair Ave E., Ste. 1010
Toronto, ON, Canada M4T 2S3
(416) 413-9822
(416) 961-7011 Fax
www.franchiorlawyer.com
70%

Morrison Cohen Singer &
  Weinstein, LLP
750 Lexington Ave.
New York, NY 10022
(212) 735-8872
(212) 735-8708 Fax
Howard Wolfson
hwolfson@mcsw.com
50%

Nelson Mullins Riley &
  Scarborough, LLP
PO Box 11070
Columbia, SC 29211
(802) 376-9533
(802) 255-9075 Fax
William H. Latham, partner
whl@nmrs.com
www.nmrs.com
50%

Kenneth G. Protonentis, P.A.
1591 Gulf Blvd., Penthouse 2
Clearwater, FL 33767
(727) 596-3435
(727) 596-2076 Fax
ken.pro@gte.net
100%

Weston Patrick Williard &
Redding, PA
84 State St.
Boston, MA 02109
(617) 742-9310
(617) 742-5734 Fax
L. Seth Stadfeld
www.franchiscounsel.com
90%

Zarco & Pardo, P.A.
NationsBank Tower, 100 SE 2 St.,
27th Floor
Miami, FL 33131
(305) 374-5418
(305) 374-5428 Fax
Robert M. Einhorn, managing
partner
www.zarcopardo.com
90%

Business Capital Lenders

The following lenders focus highly on either the restaurant or franchise community, or both. Dollar amounts refer to deal ranges.

American Commercial Capital LLC
5963 LaPlace Court, Ste. 300
Carlsbad, CA 92008
(760) 918-2700
(760) 918-2727 Fax
www.accaptial.com
Marc Furstein, managing director
$1-100 million

AMRESCO
700 N. Pearl St., Ste. 1900
Dallas, TX 75201

(800) 307-5363
(214) 953-7794 Fax
www.amresco.com
Marvin Franklin, managing director
$500,000-25 million

The Associates
300 E. Carpenter Freeway, Ste. 1250
Irving, TX 75062
(972) 652-3324
(972) 652-3340 Fax
www.sbf-franchise.com
Jeannie Baldwin, senior business
development officer
jeannie_baldwin@afcc.com
$150,000-1.5 million

Atherton Capital Inc.
1001 Bayhill Dr., Ste. 155
San Bruno, CA 94066
(800) 277-4232
(650) 827-7950 Fax
www.atherton.net
info@atherton.net
$350,000-1.75 million

BB & T Capital Markets
PO Box 1575
Richmond, VA 23218
(804) 780-3242
(804) 649-2615 Fax
Jim Sowers, vice president
jsowers@scottstringfellow.com
$10 million-100 million

Banco Popular
7 West 51 St.
New York, NY 10019
(212) 445-1821
(212) 265-4827 Fax
www.bancopopular.com

Agustin Mas, senior vice president
amas@bppr.com
Up to $2 million

Bank United
3200 Southwest Freeway
Houston, TX 77027
(919) 839-5511
(919) 839-0706 Fax
www.bankunited.com
David White, president SBA
 lending
dwhite7518@aol.com
$250,000-3.5 million

Business Lenders
15 Lewis St.
Hartford, CT 06103
(860) 244-9202
(860) 527-0884 Fax
www.businesslenders.com
Judy Hart, senior vice president
jhart@businesslenders.com
$100,000-3 million

Business Loan Express
645 Madison Ave., 19th Floor
New York, NY 10022
(800) SBA-LOAN
(212) 888-3949 Fax
www.sbaloans.com
Jodi Polonet, director of marketing
info@businessloanexpress.net
Up to $3 million

Captec Financial Group, Inc.
24 Frank Lloyd Wright Dr., Lobby
 L., 4th Floor
Ann Arbor, MI 48106-0544
(800) 522-7832
(734) 214-2701 Fax
www.captec.com

H. Reid Sherard, senior vice president sales and marketing
franchisegroup@captec.com
Minimum $75,000

The CIT Group, Inc.
650 CIT Drive.
Livingston, NJ 07039
(973) 422-6052
(973) 422-6054 Fax
www.cit.com
George Keith, VP business
 development
george.keith@cit.com
$250,000-50 million

Citicapital
2600 Michelson Dr., Floor 12
Irvine, CA 92612
(800) 285-CITI (2484)
(949) 250-6990 Fax
www.citicorp.com/gef
$1 million-no upper limit

Top 25 Chains Ranked by 2000 Sales

Company	Sales	Units
Pizza Hut	$7.3b	12,084
Domino's	3.543b	7,000
Papa John's	1.7b	2,625
Little Caesars	1.14b	3,900
Sbarro	548m	599
Tony Roma's	401m	NR
Chuck E. Cheese	388.6m	380
Round Table	365m	539
Pizzeria Uno	339.9m	177
Godfather's	315m	592
CiCi's	301m	354
Papa Murphy's	260m	640
California Pizza Kitchen	248m	112
Piccadilly Circus	225m	930
Boston Pizza	205m	142
Mazzio's	175m	254
Pizza Inn	173m	420
Pizza Pizza	160m	320
Bertucci's	143.9m	73
Donato's	135m	166
Peter Piper	130m	146
Double Double	117m	113
Papa Gino's	115.4m	172
Mr. Gatti's	115m	170
LaRosa's	96m	50

Definitions of Terms

Administrative and General Expenses:
Those expenses necessary to operate the business but not directly related to customer service.

American with Disabilities Act (ADA):
A comprehensive civil rights law protecting people with disabilities.

Back of the House:
Food storage, production, and preparation areas as opposed to front of the house which is the serving and dining or "public" area.

Beer Cooler:
Cooler in which kegs, cans, or bottles of beer are refrigerated. The direct-draw cooler is a low-counter type with self-contained tapping equipment and dispensing head(s). Beer Dispenser or Tapping Cabinet. Refrigerated or ice- cooled insulated cabinet with beer or soda and/or water-dispensing heads, drainer plate, and pan recessed flush with he bar top and a drain trough under. Usually built into a liquor bar top, between workboards.

Beer System:
A method for tapping beer from remote located refrigerated kegs and transporting it through pressuri-zed, refrigerated, and insulated lines to dispensing heads located at one or more stations in the bar and/or back-bar.

Benchmark:
A standard or point of reference used to measure or judge quality, value, etc.

Bid:
Financial and/or operating proposal submitted to an individual or company requesting the opportunity to provide a given service and/or product.

Branded Concepts:
Nationally or regionally trade-marked concepts that can be incorporated into a foodservice program for a franchise or licensing fee.

Branding:
A marketing strategy that takes consumer-recognized (or perceived recognized) restaurant and food manufacturer brands, and utilizes brand equity to build traffic, expand sales, increase share, grow availability, establish food credibility, improve satisfaction, raise the profile of the foodservice program and increase profits.

Breakeven Point:
The point where the sum of all costs equals sales; profit equals zero.

Budget:
The financial expression of a realistic statement of management's objectives and goals.

Buffalo Chopper:
A piece of kitchen equipment used for finely chopping raw or cooked products.

Buffet Unit:
One or more mobile or stationary counters having flat surfaces, with cold pans or heated wells at the top, on which chafing dishes, canape trays, or other food displays can be placed for self service.

Carbonator:
Motor-driven water pump, with tank and con-trol valves, to combine cold water and CO_2 gas in a storage tank. producing soda water. Used for soda fountains, car-bonated beverage dispensers, and dispensing systems.

Cash Drawer:
Shallow drawer located under a counter top at the cashier end. Often provided with removable com-partmented insert for currency and coins.

Catering:
To provide prearranged foodservice to the specific needs of any group .

Cental Kitchen:
Single production area where foods are prepared for and transported to multiple service areas.

Check Average:
Total dollar sales received divided by the total number of persons served.

Checkout Counter:
Counter located between a cafeteria serving area or kitchen and a dining room, for use by checker and/or cashier. Also called cashier counter.

Closing Inventory:
The actual physical count of inventory at the end of a period expressed as groups of values (units, values, etc.).

Cold Pan:
Insulated depressed pan set into a table or coun-ter top; provided with waste outlet; may be refrigerated with crushed ice, refrigeration coil fastened to the underside of the lining, or a cold plate. A perforated false bottom is provided when ice is used.

Condensate Evaporator:
honed coil through which com-pressed refrigerant flows, absorbing the heat inside refriger-ator or freezer.

Condensing Unit, Refrigeration:
Assembly consisting of mechanical compressor driven by electric-powered motor with either air or water-cooling device. (1) Open-type unit has major components separate but mounted on same base. (2) Hermetic-type unit has major components enclosed in same sealer housing, with no external shaft, and motor operating in refrigerant atmosphere. (3) Semi-hermetic-type unit has hermetically sealed compressor whose housing is sealed and has means of access for servicing internal parts in field.

Condiment Shelf or Rack:
Shelf or rack mounted above or under a table top to hold several condiment items for use by the cook or baker.

Contract:
The legal agreement between a company, institution or individual (know as the client) and a professional foodservice contracting company (Known as the contractor) to provide foodservice based on the specifications of the submitted proposal.

Contract Cleaning:
A service contractor for night cleaning, extermination, hood/ventilator cleaning.

Contracted Foodservice:
A foodservice operation which is provided by an independent contractor on a predetermined fee basis.

Contracted Vending:
A vending operation which is installed and operated by an independent contractor. The contractor retains title to the vending equipment. Controllable Expenses. The total of all payroll costs, direct operating, advertising/promotion, utilities, administrative and general, repair and maintenance expenses.

Controllable Cost:
A short-term change that can be effected by management, such as food cost, labor cost, etc.

Convection Oven:
Gas- or electric-heated. Heat is circu-lated through the oven interior with fan or blower system. Interior may be equipped with racks and/or shelves. Ovens may be stacked or set on stand. Oven bottom may be con-structed as part of the platform of a mobile basket rack cart.

Conventional Oven:
An oven with the heat source, either gas or electric, located beneath the deck; air is indirectly circulated.

Conveyor Ovens:
The oven is set at one temperature and the conveyor line is timed so that the desired product is baked consistently each and every time.

Cook-Chill:
The process of fully or partially cooking food then rapidly chilling it from the cooking temperature to below 40 F. degrees in two hours or less.

C - Stores:
Cash-and-carry convenience stores that vend a variety of sundries and groceries.

Cooker and Kettle, Combination:
One or more steam -jacketed kettles with one or more steam cookers mounted in top of single cabinet base or tops of adjoining cabinet bases. May be for direct steam operation or provided with steam coil, gas- or electric-heated steam generator in the base under the steam cooker(s).

Cost/benefit Ratio:
The relationship between costs incurred in implementing and maintaining a control or control system and the benefits of monetary savings derived from doing so.

Cost of Sales:
The total dollar amount of all food and beverage used in a particular month or accounting period.

Cover:
A customer in a dining facility.

Cross-training:
Teaching a worker to perform the duties of some job or jobs other then his own.

Cut Table:
The area, usually a stainless steel table, where pizzas are pulled from the oven, cut and either packaged for carryout or delivery or handed to servers for dine-in orders.

Demographics:
A statistical evaluation process whereby the total available population is segmented according to certain factors such as geographic location, age,

sex and position in the work force. In B&I, demographics usually refer to sex, exempt/nonexempt, age, group, work shift.

Dicing Machine:
Bench-mounted hand- or motor-driven two-operation machine that first forces food through a grid network of knives in a square pattern and then slices the food the same length as the side of the square. May be attached to food mixing or cutting machine. Also called dicing attachment or cubing machine.

Dish Cart:
Cart for storage and dispensing of clean or soiled dishes. Usually of height to roll under counter or table top.

Dish Dispenser:
A spring-activated devise which raises stacks of plates or loaded warewashing racks to service level position. May be built into another piece of equipment or free standing portable. Also available in heated units.

Dish Table:
Work surface with raised sides and end(s) having its surface pitched to a built-in waste outlet, adjoin-ing a sink or warewashing machine. There may be a soiled table used for receiving, sorting, and racking ware, located at load end of the sink or washing machine, and a clean table at unload end for draining of rinse water, drying, and stacking ware.

Dispenser:
Unit for storage and dispensing of beverages, condiments, food, and ware. May be insulated and refriger-ated or heated. May be provided with self-leveling device. May be counter- or floor-mounted, stationary or mobile.

Display Case:
A semi- or fully enclosed case of one or more shelves, mounted on counter top or wall, for display of desserts. Semi-enclosed types have transparent end panels and sneeze guards along customers' side to protect uncov-ered foods. Refrigerated types have insulated transparent panels and doors. Heated types are usually provided with sliding doors

and electric heating units, with or without humidifier.

Dolly:
Solid platform or open framework mounted on a set of casters, for storage and transportation of heavy items. May be equipped with handle or push bar.

Dough Divider:
Motor-driven floor-type machine to divide dough (usually for bread) into equally scaled pieces. Pieces are removed from work surface by conveyor to next operation. Normally used for bread dough. Also called bread divider.

Dough Mixer:
(1) Motor-driven machine with vertical spin-dle to which various whips and beaters are attached. Bowl is raised to the agitator. Mixers of 5- to 20-quart capacity are bench mounted. Mixers of 20- to 140-quart capacity are floor type. (2) Motor-driven, floor-type horizontal machine with tilting-type bowl and horizontal agitator(s) for a large dough batch. Also called kneading machine or mixer.

Dough Retarder:
May be upright reach-in, low-counter bench-type, or walk-in refrigerator with series of racks or tray slides and/or shelves, in which dough is kept cool, to retard rising.

Dough Rounder:
Motor-driven floor-mounted machine into which a piece of dough is dropped and rounded to ball shape by means of a rotating cone and fixed spiral raceway running from top to bottom. See Roll Divider.

Dough Sheeter:
Motor- or hand-driven machine with a series of adjustable rollers to roll dough to sheets of even thickness. Also called pie crust roller.

Dough Trough:
Large tub with tapered sides, usually mounted on casters, for storing and transporting large batches of dough. Some troughs have gates at the ends for pouring dough when the trough is lifted above a divider and tilted.

Dram Shop Laws:
State statutes holding the serving establishment and the server liable for damages to others resulting from the serving of alcoholic beverages to intoxicated customers.

Drop-in Unit:
Any warming, cooling, cooking, or storage unit that is dropped into an opening in a counter or table top and is fitted with accompanying mounting brackets and sized flange.

Dual Temp Refrigerator:
A combination refrigerator-freezer.

Dunnage Rack:
Mobile or stationary solid or louvered platform used to stack cased or bagged goods in a storeroom or walk-in refrigerator or freezer.

Dupe:
Short for "duplicate", as in "dupe tickets".

Durable Equipment:
Permanent pieces of equipment used in preparation, service or storage.

ECR:
Electronic cash registers which have the capability of maintaining detailed information on all product sales.

EDP:
Electronic Data Processing. Employee Feeding - Foodservice provided in an industrial or institutional setting. Also called implant feeding, this term makes no distinction between company operated and contracted operations.

E-Coli:
A bacteria found in raw meat and dairy which, when transmitted to the human body, can result in serious illness or, in some cases, death.

Entree:
A dish served as the main course of a meal.

Ethnic Foods:
Food normally associated with certain nationalities or religious groups.

Expendable Equipment:
Items which must be periodically replaced because of loss or breakage; such as chinaware, flatware, kitchen utensils. Commonly referred to as smallwares.

FIFO:
Stands for First In, First Out; a rotating method for inventory, usually perishable products, where the first product delivered for usage and storage is the first used.

Fixed Expenses:
Basic costs which remain constant and do not fluctuate with increases or decreases in sales and/or volume. Examples are depreciation, rent or square footage charges, management fees.

Flatware:
Knife, spoon, and fork used by the diner.

Floor Scale:
(1) Unit fixed in a pit, its platform flush with finished floor. May have dial or beam mounted on top of the housing at the rear of platform framing, plus tare beam. Used for weighing heavy objects on mobile carriers. (2) Mobile type. See Platform Scale.

Food Cost:
The ratio of dollars of food purchased to revenue, expressed as a percentage. Unless certain paper products are directly related with the service of food (such as disposable plates, cartons, etc.), they should not be included in food cost.

Food Cutter:
(1) Motor-driven bench- or floor-mounted machine with a rotating shallow bowl to carry food through a set of rotating horizontal knives whose axis is perpendicu-lar to the radii of the bowl. Knives are set under hinged-up cover. (2) Motor-driven floor-mounted high-speed machine with vertical tilting bowl having a vertical shaft with rotat-ing knife.

Also called vertical cutter/mixer or sold under various brand names.

Food Merchandiser:
Refrigerated, heated, or non-insulated case or cabinet with transparent doors and possibly transpar-ent ends. Used for display and sometimes self-service of foods.

Food Poisoning:
The name for the gastrointestinal symptoms caused by a poison or a toxin released into the food, often by an offending bacteria.

Food Shaper:
(1) Motor-driven unit with loading hopper, bench or floor mounted. Shapes food into rectangular or round patties of varying thickness. May be equipped with paper interleaving, removing, and conveying devices. (2) Attachment to meat chopper to shape ground food into rectangles of varied thickness. Also called food former.

Food Slicer:
Equipment designed for slicing meat, cheese, vegetables. Can be adjust-ed for varying slice thicknesses for accurate portion control.

Food Warmer:
(1) Insulated mobile or stationary cabinet with shelves, racks, or tray slides, having insulated doors or drawers. May be electric, steam or gas heated and provided with humidity control. (2) Infrared lamp or elec-tric radiant heating element with or without a glass enclosure, mount-ed above the serving unit in a hot-food section.

Free-hand:
Not using portion-control devices, such as portion cups, for any prod-uct, particularly pizza. Also referred to as eyeballing or freestyle.

Front Of The House:
The serving and dining pr "public" area of a foodservice facility.

Fryer:
Floor- or bench-mounted unit heated by gas or elec-tricity with tank of oil or At into which foods are immersed. Common type has deep tank.

Special types have shallow tanks for fish, chicken, doughnuts, etc., and basket-conveyor type has a shallow tank for draining with baskets, arms, mesh-type belt, or rotating auger to move foods through the bath. Pressure type has a lift or hinged cover to seal the top of the fryer tank.

Furnishings:
Items such as tables, chairs, carpeting and draperies which must be replaced more frequently than durable equipment but less frequently than expendable equipment.

General Insurance:
All types of insurance not related to employee benefits or extended coverage on the premises or contents including, security, fraud/forgery, fidelity bonds, public liability, food poisoning, use and occupancy, lost or damaged articles, and partner's or officer's life insurance.

Grater:
(1) Bench mounted hand- or motor-driven machine in which food is forced against the Lice of a revolving grater plate by a pusher or hopper plate. (2) Part of vegetable -slicing attachment to food machine.

Grill:
Bench-mounted unit with fixed lower and hinged upper electrically heated plates. Plates have a waffle pattern for waffles, grooves for steaks, and are smooth for sandwiches.

Gross Margin:
Unit price minus unit cost OR total sales minus total cost.

Gross Sales:
All revenue less applicable sales tax.

Guest Check:
Acts either or both as an itemized invoice or receipt for a patron's food and drink order.

Ice Dispenser:
A floor-, counter-, or wall-mounted station-ary ice storage bin with motor-driven agitator and conveyor mechanism or gravity feed, that dis-

penses a measure of ice (cubed or crushed) through a discharge chute into a con-tainer at working level.

Ice Maker:
Floor-, counter-, or wall-mounted unit containing refrigeration machinery for making cubed, flaked, and crushed ice. Maker may have integral ice storage bin. Larger-capacity machines generally have a separate bin in which ice is received via a connecting chute. Capacity is rated in pounds of ice per twenty-four-hour day.

Infrared Heater or Warmer:
Unit consisting of one or more lamps or electric strip heaters, with or without protective covering or reflector, mounted in a bracket or housing. Usually set over hot-food serving and display a sensor inside enclosed displays. Unit produces infrared heat to keep food warm.

Infrared Oven:
Oven having heat generated and radiated from electric infrared heating elements encased in a glass tube or from an exposed quartz infrared plate.

Insert:
Rectangular pan or round pot set into the top of a steam or hot food table.

Inventory Turnover:
The ratio of cost of food or beverages sold to average inventory of food or beverages for a period.

Irradiation:
A method of preservation in which a radiation source is used to eliminate bacterial contamination and sterilize or pasteurize the food and/or spices.

Knife Rack:
Slotted wood or stainless steel bar set away and attached to edge of table top or butcher block. This forms a slot into which cutlery blades are inserted and held up by handles of same while the handles protrude at the top.

Knife Sharpener:
(1) Bench-mounted motor-driven ma-chine with rotating stones forming a V to grind edges on both sides of a blade. (2) Attachment to slicing machine. (3) Grinding-wheel attachment to food machine, having an attachment hub.

Licenses & Permits:
Federal, state and municipal licenses including any special permits or inspection fees.

Low-Calorie:
40 calories or fewer per serving.

Low-Cholesterol:
20 milligrams or fewer and two grams or fewer of saturated fat per serving.

Low-Fat:
Three grams or fewer per serving.

Low-Sodium:
140 milligrams or fewer per serving.

Make Table (or Make Line):
The area in the back-of-the-house where product is prepared (pizzas topped) and then placed in the oven. Kitchens with multiple make stations divide up the specific stations (i.e., sandwich line or station, pasta line or station, etc.).

Manning Chart:
A chart which graphically illustrates the projected labor requirements for an operation, showing the number of cafeteria employees, their function and time schedule.

Manual Foodservice:
A facility in which foods and services are provided by human labor.

Marketing:
Includes all selling and promotion costs, direct mail, donations, souvenirs, favors, advertising, public relations and publicity, franchise fees

and royalties or commissions and market research (surveys).

Marketing Segmentation:
The identification of particular groups within the available customer base by applying factors such as sex, age, exempt/non-exempt, work shift. See Demographics.

Meat Chopper:
Table- or floor-mounted hand- or motor-driven horizontal machine. Food placed in top-mounted hopper is fed by a stomper into cylinder with tight-fitting auger to drive food against rotating knife and perforated plate. Also called meat grinder.

Menu Board:
Sign with fixed or changeable letters, or removable lines listing the food items and prices.

Menu Cycle:
Repeating an established menu in a predetermined rotation. Generally, this is done every four or five weeks.

Menu Explosion:
A process for determining the amount of each item on a menu that will usually prepared in a specific kitchen. Done to determine the size of equipment necessary in a new or remodeled kitchen.

Menu Matrix:
Establishes the "sales mix" of product sold and is used to determine food costs.

Menu Pattern or Plan:
A listing of the number of entrees, vegetables, salads, desserts, and beverages that will be offered for sale at each meal period.

Merchandising:
Any marketing or promotional technique which is designed to stimulate sales. May encompass food displays, platter presentations, use of promotional materials distributed by processors and manufacturers, or use of merchandising materials prepared in-house.

Mixer, Food:
Motor-driven machine with vertical spindle having several speeds on which various whips and beaters are mounted. Bowl is raised up to agitator. Mixers of 5- to 20-quart capacity are bench type. Mixers of 20- to 1 40-quart capacity are floor type.

Mixer Stand:
Low-height stationary or mobile stand with four legs and a solid top to support a mixer up to 20-quart size. May be provided with under shelf and vertical rack for mixer parts.

Mixer, Vertical Cutter:
See Vertical Cutter/Mixer.

Modular Equipment:
Equipment all the same design, height and color which can be used fee standing or in any combination.

Modular Stand:
Low-height open stationary stand with four or more legs, having an open framework top, to support heavy-duty modular cooking equipment.

Oven:
Fully enclosed insulated chamber with gas-, electric-, or oil-fired heat, provided with thermostatic control. Deck-type units have chambers or sections stacked one above the other. Bake-type decks are approximately 7 inches high inside. Roast-type decks are 12 to 14 inches high inside.

Oven Production:
Items which have been prepared but not sold or consumed at the conclusion of the meal for which they were produced.

Payroll Tax & Benefits:
Payroll taxes; FICA, Fula, state unemployment and state health insurance, social insurance (i.e.., worker's compensation insurance, welfare or pension plan payments, accident and health insurance premiums and the cost of employee instruction and education, employees parties, and employee meals.)

Per Capita Spending:
Total dollar sales received over a specified period of time divided by the total available population (not the actual number of foodservice participants.)

Point of Sale:
The point at which food and beverage is transferred to a customer. Often cash registers are referred to as point-of-sale units.

Portion-Pak:
Pre-packaged, individual servings of condiments in disposable packaging.

Potentialized Food Cost:
The ideal food cost (given a defined menu matrix) which corresponds to the mix. A potentialized food cost is used to compare with the actual food cost to determine areas of variance.

Pizza Oven:
Baking-type oven of one or more decks, gas, electric, or oil fired, having temperature range from 350¡ to 700¡F. Deck(s) are of heat-retaining masonry material. Pizza Sheeter. See Dough Sheeter.

Prefabricated Cooler:
Walk-in refrigerator or freezer having insulated walls, ceiling, and floor fabricated in a shop and assembled on the job site. The insulated floor and base of the walls may be constructed as part of the building. Preparation Table or Counter. Unit located in the prepara-tion area of a kitchen, for cutting, slicing, peeling, and other preparation of foods.

Pre-portioned:
Food items which are purchased in a fully trimmed, portioned state, ready for cooking.

Prerinse or Prewash Sink:
Sink constructed as an integral part of a soiled dish table, located near a dishwashing machine, and furnished with removable perforated scrap basket(s) and spray hose.

Prewash:
Separate machine or built-in section of a ware-washing machine with

tank and pump or fresh-water supply. Pump recirculates water over ware; fresh-water type sprays over ware; before pumped wash section of machine.

Product Cost:
The combined costs of all food ingredients and items purchased from an outside source which are used to produce an item for sale.

Productivity:
Measurable amount of work produced by the workforce.

Productivity Rate:
A measure developed to determine the level of work produced by an individual or group. May be expressed as sales dollars realized per labor hour, customers served per labor hour, meals served per labor hour, etc.

Profit Limitation Contract:
An agreement which restricts a contractors profits to a set percentage of sales and/or to a predetermined dollar amount. Any excess profits are retained by the client.

Profit & Loss Contract:
A contractual arrangement whereby the contractor is responsible for the financial operation of the foodservice. The risk is placed upon the contractor to make money in the operation without a subsidy from the organization.

Profit & Loss Statements:
A formal accounting of income matched against expenses incurred in the operation of a particular facility to determine the current profit level; usually produced monthly.

Projected Profit and Loss:
A tabulation of anticipated revenues and expenses for specific operating location in order to determine potential profits.

Promotion:
Communicating to the consumer about the availability of a particular product or planned event in order to stimulate interest and increase sales.

Proposal:
A bid submitted by a contractor which includes a complete description of the type of foodservice to be provided and the fees that will be charged.

Proof Box or Cabinet:
Fully enclosed cabinet with gas, steam, or electric heater and humidifier. Sometimes unit may be insulated type with thermostatic and humidity controls. Box may be mobile. Traveling-type Proofer has a conveying mechanism inside the overhead cabinet, as in large commer-cial bread bakery.

Publicity:
An indirect effort to increase sales by making the consumer more aware of the operation. This is accomplished by creating news - something unusual, exceptional, or special about the operation - which will merit coverage by newspapers, magazines or other media.

RFB:
A Request For Bids sets all of the specifications and requirements and asked the proposing company to bid a price to perform the service or provide the products required.

RFP:
A Request For Proposals sets some of the requirements and asks the proposing company how it would propose to operate a program and for what price.

RFQ:
A Request For Qualifications simply asks for companies to submit their qualifications to perform a described level of foodservice. It is used to determine who is qualified to respond to an RFB or RFP.

Range:
Unit with heated top surface or burners that heat utensils in which foods are cooked, or cook foods directly. Some ranges are equipped with an insulated oven base. Hot or even-heat tops and fry or griddle tops are gas or oil fired or electrically heated. Open or hot-plate tops have electric or gas burners.

Reach-in Refrigerator or Freezer:
Cabinet with the refrigeration system located on top. Fans inside the cabinet circulate the air. Interior shelves are usually adjustable. Doors are located on the front of the cabinet.

Redlining:
The process of defining distinct geographical boundaries for home delivery, a management decision based on reducing the threat of harm to delivery drivers; not delivering to selected neighborhoods otherwise within a delivery area due to high crime statistics, reports or experience. Redlining is so named to signify the drawing of the boundaries of restricted areas on a delivery zone map with red pen or marker.

Refrigerator Shelves:
Shelves of wire, solid, embossed, or slotted material with reinforced hemmed edges, mounted on tubular posts with adjustable sanitary brackets. May be in stationary or mobile sections.

Replacements:
Replacement of all linen, china, glassware, flatware and kitchen utensils.

Return On Investment:
The amount of money earned after taxes in relation to the total dollar investment required to operate a specific facility. Usually expressed in percentage form.

Revolving Tray Oven:
Gas-, electric-, or oil-heated oven with a motor-driven Ferris wheel device inside having four or more balanced trays. Bake or roast pans are loaded and unloaded from a single opening with a hinged-down door. Steam may be added for humidity requirements of products.

Rotary Oven:
An oven with one or more racks or shelves which rotate to assure even cooking.

Running Rate:
The current average rate for a cost category, computed over a period of time.

Salad Case:
Unit consisting of a refrigerated counter with refrigerated food pans set into the top, and a refrigerated or nonrefrigerated display case mounted on the counter top.

Salary & Wages:
Include the salaries and wages, extra wages, overtime, vacation pay, and any commission or bonuses paid to employees.

Salamander:
A backshelf or cabinet mounted over the rear of a range or steam table, absorbing the heat to keep foods on it warm.

Sales Mix:
An item-by-item and/or sales group (such as entrees, beverages, desserts, etc.) Listing showing the number and/or dollar amount sold for a specified period of time

Satellite Operation:
Point of service located away from the main preparation and/or service location. Food for a satellite operation is customarily prepared in a central kitchen, then transported by cart to the serving area.

Slicer:
Bench- or stand-mounted machine with a stationary motor-driven round knife and slice-thickness gauge plate, and reciprocating feed trough or carriage. Flat trough may have hand and/or spring-pressure feed plate. Gravity trough may have hand or automatic feed plate. Trough may be hand operated or motor driven. Slicer can be equipped with automatic stacking and conveying device.

Small Wares:
Small wares are all those items necessary to support the preparation and service of food with a per piece value of under a predetermined fixed amount. Smallwares include such items as pots, pans, serving utensils, china, glassware, serving patters/bowls, carving boards, etc.

Soda Dispenser:
(1) Part of soda-making and refrigeration system: dispensing head

attachment for mounting on a soda fountain, bar, counter, or at a waiter station, complete with drainer. (2) Enclosed cabinet, ice or mechanically refrigerated, to dispense premixed soda or combine soda water and syrup stored in a cabinet or remote tanks. (3) Floor or counter - mounted cabinet with a self-contained soda and refrigera-tion system having remote or self-contained syrup tanks.

Tempered:
Food brought from a frozen to a thawed state by holding under refrigeration for a specific period of time.

Theme Days:
Special event days which feature appropriate ethnic foods, decorations, and/or entertainment and are designed to stimulate additional customer sales participation and continuing interest.

Tracking:
Monitoring or measuring actual performance against established goals.

Utilities:
All costs of electricity, fuel, water, ice and refrigeration supplies, removal of waste, and engineering supplies.

Variance Cost:
Costs which increase or decrease in a direct line relationship to increases or decreases in sales.

Vegan:
A person who consumes only plant products, no animal flesh or by-products such as dairy and eggs.

Vegetarian:
A person who consumes only plant products and animal by-products such as eggs and dairy.

Vertical Cutter/Mixer:
Floor-type machine with a vertical tilting mixing bowl having a 25- to 80-quart capacity. The bowl is equipped with a two-speed motor and a high-speed agitator shaft at bowl bottom with cutting/mixing knife. A

hand- or motor-driven stirring and mixing shaft is fixed to the bowl's cover. A strainer basket may be included.

Walk-In Refrigerator:
Refrigerated rooms used for bulk storage of items.

Yield:
The amount of fully prepared, ready to consume food or beverage product that should result if directions for a specific recipe or procedure are properly followed.

Yield Price:
Product cost divided by product yield.

Index